Just Beyond The Door

Just Beyond the DOOR

TOMMY & KAREN DRUMM

Jabez Books

JUST BEYOND THE DOOR

Copyright © 2018 Tommy and Karen Drumm

ISBN: 9781790519873
Imprint: Independently published

Printed in the United States of America

Library of Congress – Catalogued in Publication Data

Editorial & Publishing Assistance:
Jabez Books Writer's Agency
www.Jabezbooks.com

Any people depicted in stock imagery provided by Getty Images are models, and such images are being used for illustrative purpose only. Certain stock imagery © Getty Images.

Because of the dynamic nature of the internet, any web addresses ore links contained in this book may have changed since publication and may no longer be valid.

Unless otherwise indicated all scriptural quotations are taken from the King James Version of the Bible. First published in 1611. Quoted from the KJV Classic Reference Bible. Copyright © 1983 by the Zondervan Corporation.

All rights reserved. No part of this publication may be reproduced, distributed, or transmitted in any form or by any means, including photocopying, recording, or other electronic or mechanical methods, without the prior written permission of the publisher, except in the case of brief quotations embodied in critical reviews and certain other noncommercial uses permitted by copyright law.

For more information and bonus material visit:
www.tdministries.com

Acknowledgements

I would like to thank some of the wonderful people who supported me and my family during my illness. People who prayed for and gave us assistance throughout this season in our lives. They gave unselfishly while I was in the hospital and rehab.

But first and foremost, I would like to thank my Lord and Savior Jesus Christ, who is the head of my life and the lifter of my head! There are no words in the English language that can express my gratitude. Lord, I am alive because of You. I am able to play music and preach again because of You! It is to You I give all the glory!

Thank you to my physicians and the nurses who went to college and worked hard to learn your specialty. I appreciate the persistence they had to keep going as God used their abilities and knowledge to keep me alive. I will always be grateful!

To Michael Pippin and Level Seven Graphics, Inc., thanks for your creativity in designing a cover for this project that reflected just what I wanted. Your work and dedication have been an inspiration.

To Lauren Bush and LB Gallery, thank you so much for your picture editing. There is no other photographer better than you. Your love for us is overwhelming.

To Rhonda Smith and Tammy Charmane, thank you for your editing skills in this project. Rhonda, you will always be my Baby-Derr.

To Dr. Cindy Trimm, thank you for believing in me. You have been a light for those who have listened to your heart. I am an ear to your words of wisdom, and I certainly appreciate your love and anointing. Thank you for praying for me and my family. I will forever be grateful.

Thank you to my best friends, Jody Rogers and Milton Spears, and my in-laws, Bill and Velda Heaston, for being at my side and never letting go of the faith they have. You were there through the brain surgeries, and the years of healing and recovery. Thank you also for standing at the wailing wall with my wife and son.

Thank you to Todd Clinard, my best friend and Associate Pastor; and his wife Kristie, who were, during this time, working at the hospital where I was sent. If they had not obeyed the call of God to move from Florida to Dallas in 2003, they would not have been there to be used by God to position me with the right doctors and the right hospital. I would not have made it without you, and I love you both with all my heart for it! Romans 8:28 says, "And we know that all things work together for good to them who love the Lord, to them who are the called according to His purpose."

To my son, Joshuia, who held himself together at the age of 15 and stood with his mother to proclaim healing over my life, I love you! It was a hard road, but we made it. The experience we have been through together as a family positioned you to be able to minister to others during their great times of need. You have walked where many people are walking and you have hurt where many people are hurting. God will use it all to bring glory to His name. I am proud of the man you are becoming. I am so glad He chose me to be your father. I love you more than words can express.

And finally, through all the time we had to walk by faith and not by feelings, I want to tell my wife, Karen, thank you! You prayed for me in the night; you stood for me, with me, and through the darkest hour of our lives. All I can say is, I thank God for His sweet grace through brain surgery and recovery. I am so grateful you were there with me through it all. Thank you for your love with dedicated commitment to our marriage and to God. I love you more than words can express.

Tommy Drumm

FOREWORD BY
Dr. Cindy Trimm

Many people don't like to think about death; however, the current death rate is 100%. Worldwide 2 people die every second, 105 every minute, and nearly 6,316 every hour. This means that approximately 151,600 individuals daily make Heaven or Hell their home. [1]

Most people who consider death have no understanding of what happens after death. However, if Heaven is to be an eternal home, it would be wise to gain an understanding of what's on the other side. Pastors Tommy and Karen Drumm's account of their amazing experience does just that.

Jesus intentionally used words with physical details (mansion, place) as he communicated where he was going and what he established for us. He wanted to wet our appetite and relieve any negative ideas, interpretations or doubts about what we had to look forward to.

---

[1] http://www.ecology.com/birth-death-rates/

"In My Father's house are many mansions; if *it were* not *so*, I would have told you. I go to prepare a place for you." [2]

Perhaps you've come to this book taxed, burdened, baffled, discouraged, disheartened or even traumatized. You may have lost a loved one recently and have a concern about their eternal existence and new home. Maybe you've simply become skeptical or have lost hope.

If so, Pastor Drumm's experience as captured in this book will be of profound importance to you. It is a careful, eyewitness account of a life-changing experience that is reassuring and biblically based. It substantially describes Heaven and is poised to bring peace and resolve any doubts and concerns.

We can all learn a great deal from what Pastor Drumm saw and reported and what his wife, Prophetess Karen, experienced through the powerful corridors of prayer and interactions with those who were Spirit-filled and focused during this pivotal time in their lives.

May *Just Beyond the Door* increase your passion for living a

---

[2] John 14:2

full and meaningful life and give you hope for the future.

You don't have to live in a fog of questions as it relates to the incredible place He promised is prepared for us. Pastors Tommy and Karen's remarkable story helps us to see through the fog and picture the shore, our eternal home, Heaven. If you're weary and don't know how you can keep going, I pray this book will help you see the shore.

CONTENTS

Acknowledgements

Foreword by Dr. Cindy Trimm

Chapter 1:	Cultivating Faith (Karen)	15
Chapter 2:	Warning Signs (Tommy)	29
Chapter 3:	The Bleed (Karen)	33
Chapter 4:	The Covenant (Karen)	45
Chapter 5:	God Blocked It (Karen)	60
Chapter 6:	A Fork In The Road (Tommy)	74
Chapter 7:	Faith Was In Charge (Karen)	77
Chapter 8:	The Shift (Karen)	82
Chapter 9:	Anew (Karen)	92
Chapter 10:	Prayer of Obedience (Karen)	102
Chapter 11:	The Promise (Karen)	108
Chapter 12:	The Confirmation (Karen)	115

Chapter 13:	The Arrival (Tommy)	130
Chapter 14:	Three Angels (Tommy)	145
Chapter 15:	The Estate (Tommy)	155
Chapter 16:	The Promise Land (Tommy)	160
Chapter 17:	I See Him (Tommy)	169
Chapter 18:	His Eyes (Tommy)	176
Chapter 19:	The Wait (Karen)	182
Chapter 20:	God Covers Us (Karen)	190
Chapter 21:	He Turned It (Karen)	203
Chapter 22:	Possessing My Authority (Karen)	212
Chapter 23:	Authentic Miracles (Karen)	221
Chapter 24:	It Is Your Turn	225

Medical Side And Report (Todd Clinard)   239

Chapter 1

Cultivating Faith

Karen

As we go through life, dreams, visions and desires are developed. And throughout the development stages of these components, we rarely anticipate the setbacks of heartache, trouble and even death that might occur. Yes, we all have faced circumstances from time to time that we never expected. We certainly don't always anticipate things that can make it so difficult that we want to give up.

Life is full of unexpected experiences that can either bring us joy or sadness, failures and successes. Our daily decisions will either make or break us. Our attitude and our mindset will be pillars of strength or crutches we lean on "when trouble comes knocking at our door."

Your reactions to hurt or anger can change the trajectory of your life forever, and if not handled properly, you will repeat the lesson in life again. Whatever you give yourself to—the pillars or the crutches—will determine the outcome of your life, whether you will be thriving or surviving.

If we allow ourselves to walk in faith, when adversities arise, eventually mountains will be moved and obstacles will be destroyed. Jesus said,

"If you have the faith as the size of
a grain of a mustard seed and speak to this
mountain to be removed and do not doubt
within your heart, it will be moved."
(Mark 11:23 Amplified)

Faith causes you to trust in God. Faith will cause your reaction to be what it needs to be when we are "slapped in the face" with all the difficulties life brings.

Whatever our decision ends up being, when it is made with

> *As I walked toward the room, drawn by the anointing, I saw a young man playing the piano and singing. It was Tommy Drumm. At the time, I had no idea he would be the man with whom I would spend the rest of my life.*

trust in God, it will bring growth to our lives and will take us to a new level. As we reach to achieve the destiny God has for us, we should always come out of it with experience. God wants us to learn from it.

Even if we make the wrong choice in life, we learn from it. A positive or negative outlook will determine our outcome. The problems we go through have caused us to gain the knowledge on how we should respond in hard times. Our response will eventually give us the results for which we are looking.

Tommy and I have had experiences over the last ten years which have become a huge part of our story (part of our lives), and we want to share them with you. My hope is to bring you help, strength and encouragement, that your faith would be increased and that your joy might be full.

The Beginning of Us

In January 1987, Tommy and I met in Baton Rouge, Louisiana, at Jimmy Swaggart Bible College. I will never forget the day I met him. I was a student and living on campus. One day after going out with friends I was walking back to my dorm I heard someone playing the piano and it was different. It was not like all the times I had heard everyone else playing. There was a different sound. A different feel. It stimulated a unique feeling that spoke to the deep part inside of me and it was calling to me.

It was the anointing; something I knew from my childhood. It brought back those sweet old memories I had of growing up. It reminded me of those Sunday night services and hearing my grandfather pray. It took me back to my grandparents' house in Greely, Colorado. Every day at one o'clock, my grandfather, Reverend Melvin Brandt, would shut himself away in his study. You could hear him pray all through the house. Many times he would spend over an hour in prayer before God. It is something that once you have experienced it, you will never forget it.

As I walked toward the room, drawn by the anointing, I saw a young man playing the piano and singing. It was Tommy Drumm. At the time, I had no idea he would be the man with whom I would spend the rest of my life with.

As we began to talk, we realized we both were raised under the same type of anointing. We both were brought up knowing who God really is. He shared how God had called him to be an evangelist. I was excited, because I knew that was what the Lord had for me as well.

As we continued to talk, we realized we shared a class together, and after this encounter, we became friends. It was an outreach class that gave us all personal training for the field which we were called into. Once a week, the students would go to different churches and experience outreach and preaching.

We saw God do so much. Tommy was really the only student at the time who knew how to preach. Everyone else was still learning. So, he would preach, and we would all help pray for the people.

We went to one church where the pastor asked if the students could come back throughout that week. We were dedicated to helping people experience God, and that is exactly what was happening. So, each night we would go back and forth from our college in Baton Rouge to the Church in Mississippi. It would take us about three hours each way.

I will never forget the night we had to take two separate cars of students to go minister. The Lord really moved where young people gave their hearts to God in the service. At the end of the service we all climbed back into the cars and headed back to school.

We were in the car talking about all the things God had done that night and how strongly we could feel His presence. We were caught up in singing, laughing and enjoying our feelings of accomplishments.

However, the unlit, two-lane, blacktop road made the night trip even darker. We were in an area where there were no lights from the houses or even a town. We could not see anything out of the side windows of the car because of the darkness of night. On top of all of that, it was so cloudy, the moon did not shine at all. We could barely see the road in front of us.

Both drivers were traveling about 80 miles an hour, when suddenly we could see a little tiny flashing of light in front of us moving back and forth. At first, we could not tell what it was, because it was so dark; suddenly we could see a large bus backing out of a very dark parking lot onto the blacktop road. The back half of the bus was in the middle of the road as we were swiftly approaching, and before we knew it, we slipped very quickly between the bus and the large ditch on the right side of us.

We quickly stopped, knowing the carload behind us was probably talking of the goodness of God and not seeing that tiny flashlight either. The bus never stopped backing up. By now it was across both lanes of the road. With no time to get out and warn the people to move the bus forward, we screamed, "JESUS! JESUS!"

We could see the car coming, driving as fast as we had been. Then, it was as if God took His hands and stretched the road out. The car SLIPPED between the bus and the ditch. I STILL DO NOT KNOW HOW THAT HAPPENED, BUT GOD! The car came to a stop and everyone got out shocked, amazed, and so grateful for the goodness and mercies of God. It was nothing but God's mercy.

I have seen God do the phenomenal. I have seen the power of God do extraordinary things in my lifetime, and during my courtship with Tommy, it was no different.

After dating a couple of years, Tommy asked me to marry him. So, on October 20, 1989, we were married in Dallas, Texas. After seeing God do so many amazing things, we were excited to see what He was going to do in our lives together. We both believed God had His hands on our lives and we knew He would allow us to be a part

> *We have seen the power of God move many, many times. It caused our faith to grow to greater measures of faith. We have no idea what our tomorrow holds, but it is so important to be prepared for whatever we might wake up to.*

of Him healing the sick and the brokenhearted. Our hearts' desire was to see Him set people free from their bondages in life. We wanted to be able to share all of God's blessings with others. This was our true hearts' desire.

We began going from church to church, preaching revivals and one-night services sharing how wonderful Jesus is and all He could do. We saw many miracles and lives that were saved and changed.

Once, while Tommy was preaching, some people came running in, crying out for someone to come quickly. Their mother had just passed away. Tommy left the platform during the church service and ran next door and prayed for the woman. As the paramedic watched with amazement, the woman came back to life. Everyone that night saw a miracle happen before their very own eyes. We have seen marriages restored, barren wombs opened, and broken relationships restored. We have seen the power of God move many, many times. It caused our faith to grow to greater measures of faith.

We have no idea what our tomorrow holds, but it is so important to be prepared for whatever we might encounter.

Sometimes life sends us through a process which makes us able to handle whatever may come in our future. If you do not keep yourself committed to finding out who Jesus really is, trust me, the storm will be much harder to bear when it comes. I never stopped pursuing Him, and as a couple, we kept growing through whatever "life brought to our door" from day to day.

As I already shared, we were both raised in homes that already taught the gift of faith. I am so glad our foundation of faith was laid many years ago because over the course of time, our roots of faith grew deeper and deeper.

Being strategic is very important for the mission God has given us for our lives. It comes by actively growing in Him, reading His word, and communing with Him in prayer.

One thing we learned is the Lord will use experiences in our lives to prepare us to respond well to what is to come. I remember taking a trip with some friends to go snow skiing in Colorado. We were so excited to have some time off to enjoy ourselves in the snow. Just like anyone else, we could not wait to get in the cabin and enjoy a cup of hot chocolate, and my favorite, watch the snow fall.

On our way to the mountains, we stopped at an outlet mall. We thought maybe we could find new snow boots and gloves. While we were shopping, Tommy came in the store where I was shopping and said, "Something just happened to me. I just blew this out of my nose."

With a puzzled look, I stared at him as he held up a piece of tissue with something the size of a quarter and about half inch-thick laying in it. I immediately was concerned it might be serious, so we went quickly to a Quick Care.

We showed them the object in the tissue and they immediately sent us to the main hospital in Denver. By this time, we were amazed we were even having to go to the hospital on our trip. We had no fear but wanted to get the doctor's advice. As we walked into the ER, we did not know the Doctor from Quick Care had already called ahead to prepare the hospital for us. I realized this must be something very serious for the doctor to call ahead.

We did not have to wait. They took us right back to a room. The doctor came in and asked to see what we had. He was AMAZED. After examining Tommy, the doctor asked if we would be willing to wait for an hour. A specialist had just flown in for another purpose and he would really like for him to look at this. So, we waited. After much research, he came in to tell us some news that blew us away.

He said, "Tommy has blown a tumor out of his nose. It was not just any kind of tumor, but the fastest growing tumor you can have."

He continued, "It grows so fast that in one month it would have grown up into the brain and killed him."

He chuckled and told us we had just received free surgery and there was nothing wrong with Tommy at all and we were free to go. Wow, we were in total shock. A very surreal feeling came over me and I began to giggle and to thank God for the free surgery and for Tommy's life.

It is so important to always realize you must have faith as your foundation if you ever want to conquer when life hits you hard. Faith comes by hearing, and hearing the Word of God.

"So then, faith cometh by hearing, and hearing by the Word of God."

(Romans 10:17 KJV)

By October 17, 2004, we had worked in the ministry together for fifteen years. It was at this time we felt the call of God to change from traveling so much to starting a ministry in the Dallas area. We started planning and working on the vision God had given to us for a new church. Todd and Kristie Clinard, who were our new Associate Pastors, decided to leave their home and family roots in Florida to join the church ministry. We were swiftly growing and developing. It was an exciting time!

Our first services were held in a hotel conference room. After three years, we then prepared to move to a storefront. In February 2007, we began to remodel and make the storefront ready to hold services. We could not wait to get into this building to see what God was going to do next.

That unexpected *next* was a moment that launched our family and ministry into the greatest trial of our lives.

Chapter 2

Warning Signs

Tommy

In June of 2006, I went to bed one evening, tired from an exhausting day. My wife and I had only one window in our bedroom, and our curtains were dark, providing a dim, relaxing atmosphere.

There was no chance for light to come through the window at all. I had my body turned so I faced the wall. The door was closed, and the room was so dark, you could not see your hand in front of you. All of a sudden, my side of the room filled with an iridescent bluish light. It was not eerie, and I could tell that the Lord was trying to let me in on something I needed to know.

The first thought that came to me was someone close to me was about to die. After giving myself a chance to think things through, I then thought my uncle was about to pass away because we had a close relationship. I thought maybe the Lord was preparing me for his death. I also thought it might be concerning my mother since she was not in very good health. Amidst all these thoughts, suddenly deep inside, I heard, *it is me*. The Lord was warning me about *myself*.

I immediately turned my back toward this feeling, as if to say to whomever, "I am not entertaining this, and I am going to sleep." So, I did not give this experience any more thought.

I have had some people tell me it must have been a car or something that flashed its passing lights into the window, but that was not the case. There was absolutely no way for light to be in my room. Heaven was calling, and I was refusing to listen.

I am not suggesting that when God says your time is up, you can just order Him to be still, but I feel the Spirit of grace was trying to get my attention to change. At this time, I still did not fully understand. I just knew God had allowed me to see something from the heavenly realm. I did not see this light again until four weeks later when the same exact thing happened. By this time, I was evaluating myself and praying that the Lord would reveal anything I might have in my life that should not be: to forgive me and fix whatever He found inside that did not please Him.

It was during this same timeframe of the Lord showing me this light that our associate pastor's wife, Kristie, dreamed about her husband, Todd, being shot in the head. She woke up in a rage of fear for his life. When she told me what she had dreamed, I immediately knew the interpretation.

Since he was shot in the head, I asked her, "Who is his head?"

She replied, "You are his head." As his pastor, I knew it was referring me.

The head wound in her dream was not meant for Todd, but for me. We did not know at that time that the timing of her dream and the visitations I had were a warning of what was to come. Truly, there was no coincidence in all of this. God was warning, but we did not heed the signs.

It was only two weeks later I returned home from the storefront church where we were working and told my wife, "Something is wrong! Take me to the hospital."

Chapter 3

The Bleed

Karen

As we began to remodel and build the storefront as we desired, we were excited to move into the building to see what God was going to do next. We began laying new flooring and carpet along with painting the walls. Also, we had to build rooms for the nursery and offices, as well as a small platform for the front of the room. God was truly with us and the padded chairs we needed, He supplied. It was all coming together.

> *Tommy was in so much pain, I had to help him dress...but I never became concerned or fearful seeing this. I was trusting the Lord and not paying close attention to what was happening. I knew God had a plan and purpose for us and never thought this would be serious.*

Next, we agreed that February 21, 2007, would be our first night of celebration to celebrate all that God had done. It was a night we had all looked forward to for many years. Not only was this the first night of camp meeting, a weeklong series of evening services, but the celebration of our new place of worship.

Tommy and some of the church members had been working hard that day to put the finishing touches on the building. The chairs were arranged just right. The chandelier was hung, the décor was finished, and everything was perfect. Around five o'clock that evening, everything was ready, and Tommy went home to clean up for the service.

After Tommy had taken a shower, I walked into the bedroom to find him sitting on the end of the bed. As I asked what he needed ironed, he shared he had a terrible headache and was not feeling very well. My first thought was maybe his blood pressure was up from the stress of getting everything prepared for the celebration. He did not have problems with his blood pressure, but there were times it was high.

I told him to lay down for a moment while I went and got him some medicine. Before I went to get some aspirin for his headache, I felt I should call Kristie. Since she had been a nurse for many years, I knew she would have some recommendations on what to do or what could be wrong. She agreed that it could be his blood pressure as well.

Before I could get Tommy some medicine he told me I might have to preach that night. Now at that time, I was not completely developed or confident in my preaching abilities. I knew that was what God had for me, but I never really pursued mastering the skills preaching requires.

I thought to myself, *I cannot do this.*

As I continued getting ready for service, I told Tommy, "No, you will be fine. You will be able to preach."

I went ahead and ironed his clothes. I had no clue what was about to happen and never felt it was going to be serious. I really believed we would just stop by the hospital, on our way to church, to get what we needed to help him feel better.

After finishing up the last bit of ironing, I returned to the bedroom to find him still sitting on the end of the bed. He told me "Something is wrong, very wrong."

He said, as he began to move his hand back and forth on his right side to see if he could see it, "I cannot see, I cannot see on my right side. Something is wrong. I need you to take me to the hospital."

When I heard this, I knew it was serious. Although Tommy knew doctors serve a great need, he was afraid of needles and he hated shots. Tommy never liked going to the doctor and avoided them as much as possible! For him to ask to go to the hospital, I knew something was very wrong.

Also, he was in so much pain, I had to help him dress. So we quickly got dressed thinking we would go on to church after going to the hospital, but as we began to leave, all of a sudden, he felt very sick to his stomach.

By the time I got him out to the van to help him get in, I noticed he was struggling to lift his right leg up. It was becoming slower; dragging a little. I never became concerned or fearful seeing this. I just continued trusting the Lord; paying very little attention to what was happening. I knew God had a plan and purpose for us, and I never thought it was going to be serious.

During the 15-minute drive to the hospital, his condition worsen. I rolled the window down hoping the wind of the drive would help with the nausea. I still did not realize how serious this was. I thought again; perhaps, his blood pressure was probably too high. I was not fearful at all.

We arrived at the hospital at 6:30 p.m. I pulled up to the ER door, jumped out of the van and went around to Tommy's side of the van to help him get out. But by then, Tommy's right side of his body would not work. There was no way he could get out of the van on his own. I quickly ran inside to retrieve a nurse. She came out with a wheelchair and helped me get him into the chair. While I was somewhat concerned what was going on with

Tommy's body, I noticed she was not overly concerned with the signs he was showing. It was as if this really is nothing, but after sitting in the ER waiting room for a brief while, Tommy's condition continued to decline.

Finally, at 8:00 p.m. they took him from the waiting room to an examination room. I still felt we would not be there long and we would make it for the end of the service.

I remember so clearly walking back to the area where the examination rooms were. I saw a large desk area where a lot of nurses and doctors were working. They took us to a large room where two beds could fit. I could see a cabinet that had glass for its door. There were all kinds of bottles of medicine. Over the bed there was a huge light connected to a large metal arm attached to the wall. As they got Tommy on the bed, he began to tell the nurse of about his pain. Then the nurse took his vitals. His blood pressure was 210 over 100. I knew this was not good, and Tommy continued complaining of the pain in his head.

The nurse left to get him something for the pain. About five minutes later she returned with the doctor. He gave Tommy some pain medicine and ordered a CT scan. I still had no fear; I was really *trusting God*. I did not realize, at the time, but the gift of faith had taken over. I was not naïve or in denial, I simply trusted that God was going to take care of this situation. I was not concerned even after seeing how high his blood pressure was, even though I did understand it was dangerously high.

When you build the right foundation of relationship with God, it causes you to react differently to attacks of the enemy; you automatically redirect your thinking. Instead of going straight into fear, you go to God's strength—which can only come from deep inside of you, having been built up through faith. The anointing, God's Spirit, takes over.

When the doctor returned, he asked me to follow him. He took me to the monitor behind the desk where the doctors and nurses sat. He began to show me the results of Tommy's CT scan on his computer screen.

The doctor said, "Do you see this?"

I looked at a round figure on the screen. The doctor proceeded to tell me, "This is Tommy's brain."

He pointed to a shadow on the image and said, "Do you see this inside the brain?"

The shadow was as large as an orange. It was six centimeters in diameter and covered the left side and middle part of the brain.

He then said, "The shadow in the picture is a bleed on the brain."

I asked, "What does this mean?" I did not know that the left side of the brain controls the right side of the body. That was why his right leg would not work when we got to the hospital. Never in my life did I think I would be told these next words...

"The brain surgeon will be here soon to talk with you."

When he said that, I was in total shock! A brain surgeon was coming to talk to me? Was this for real? Was this really happening? I became numb.

My first thought was, *everything is going to be okay.*

I did not know how, I did not know when, but I knew Tommy was going to be fine. I did not think of tomorrow. I did not think about our future. I did not let my thoughts run wild to think of the possibilities should this go bad. I did not think of anything except I just *knew*, Jesus had us in His hands and He was going to make Tommy okay. I know some would think or say, I was in denial, but I was not, I was in faith. Faith in Christ and His Word of promise. There was such a peace that surpassed all my understanding, and it flooded over me.

> *"And the peace of God,*
> *which surpasses all understanding,*
> *will guard your hearts and minds*
> *through Christ Jesus."*
> (Philippians 4:7 KJV)

The people at church were still praying in the service that night. They did not yet know what was happening at the hospital. My first thought was, I needed to call Pastor Todd. Since he and Kristie were both in the medical field as their primary careers, I knew he would be able to answer my questions and explain everything so much better.

When I called Pastor Todd to let him know what the doctor found, he shared the information with the congregation and they all quickly came to the hospital. Over the next few hours, family and friends from all over the nation were called to pray. In the next few days, many of them traveled hundreds of miles to be with us.

One day a man with salty white hair walked in the room. He looked tired, but strong. He was over six feet tall and he introduced himself to me as Dr. Tomkins, the brain surgeon. He began to explain more to us about what was happening. The bleed on Tommy's brain was *not* a stroke; instead, it was a seepage in one of the vessels at the back-left side of the head.

I asked, "Is this due to high blood pressure?"

He said, "A bleed in this part of the brain would not be caused by blood pressure of 210 over 110." He also told us it was unheard of for this part of the brain to be affected by a bleed, and that in his entire career he had never seen this.

That is when I knew: this condition was not simply a natural physical occurrence.

You see, you must realize God has put inside each of us treasures, gifts, and greatness. The devil knows this. He wants to stop God's plan for your future and destiny by killing what has been put inside you.

This bleed could not be explained by any other reason, which lets me know the devil was trying to kill my husband, to steal his God-given future, and to destroy our lives. It does not matter who you are or where you come from, there is something on the inside of you that God has a plan and purpose for. Something that will change so many lives if the story ever gets out. If you can just realize there is something in you God is desiring to use, you will never be the same. You will know your purpose.

For I know the plans I have for you,"
declares the Lord, "plans to prosper you and not to
harm you, plans to give you hope and a future.
Then you will call on me and come and pray to me, and I will
listen to you. You will seek me and find me
when you seek me with all your heart.

(Jeremiah 29:11-13 Amplified)

Dr. Tomkins admitted Tommy into the hospital so he could put him into a drug-induced sleep. This would allow Tommy, particularly his brain, to rest until morning. The doctor was hoping for the bleed to drain on its own, which sometimes happens. So we had to wait till the next morning.

Chapter 4

The Covenant

Karen

As I rode the elevator up to the fifth floor, I had no idea what I was about to face. I was still trusting God and His promises, but I felt I just had to go through the process. I walked off the elevator, went down a small, short hallway and into a large open waiting room. The room was filled with chairs and couches placed with faux green plants to make it seem more welcoming. There was a desk with a phone on it. We had the room to ourselves.

Kristie told me, "Find a place to be comfortable, because you are going to be here a few days."

It was as if I did not hear her words. It was as if they rolled off my back. It was hard for me to embrace the suggestion that I would be there for days.

I knew I needed a place that was comfortable for the night, so I moved to a spot along the far wall where there was a couch with several chairs around it. I sat down with friends and family and thought, "Is this really happening?"

While we sat waiting to see Tommy, the hospital brought us blankets, pillows, and all kinds of snacks. Everyone got as comfortable as possible. About that time, they were checking Tommy into room five in the Critical Care Unit.

Kristie urged me to eat something and get comfortable. Food did not sound good at all, but I did take a pillow and a blanket.

The thoughts of "what if" never entered my mind. What if he does not make it or what if something happens that I am going to regret? It was as if I could not think that way. I know it had to be the Lord protecting my faith. My heart and my mind were on lockdown. I could not afford to let any negative thought or word penetrate my faith.

I have learned there are times our knowledge can make it hard to have faith. Sometimes the things we have been trained to lean on are not enough. When everything I have lean upon does not work, I tend to go to God's Word and lean on His promises, and that is exactly what I did during this ordeal; I leaned on the everlasting arms of God.

As the night unfolded, friends and ministry members continued to arrive from all over the country. Each settling in the waiting room with us. And no matter how long I had to wait, I still believed God that Tommy was going to be okay.

I shared with all our friends and family my conversation with the doctor. I *knew*! When I say, "I knew," I knew he would be completely alright.

Now, as I look back, I see how the gift of faith was working for me against the plan of the enemy. No matter what we were about to face, we knew it was going to turn out for our good.

> *"And we know that all things work together for good to those who love God, to those who are the called according to his purpose."*
> *(Romans 8:28 KJV)*

> *"To another faith by the same spirit; to another the gifts of healing by the same spirit."*
> *(1 Corinthians 12:9 KJV)*

Also, while sitting in the waiting room, one of our pastor friends shared with me a scripture that we had read earlier that day, "I have begun a good work in you and I will finish what I have started." Hearing him say this, I knew God had given me a scripture promise to stand on through this test. I knew with that scripture alone; the promise was a *"yea and amen"* moment.

When you are believing God for something, it is so important that you have a scripture you can stand on for what you are believing for from God. The scripture below is the fuel for how your faith should operate within you.

> *"Being confident of this very thing,*
> *that He who has begun a good work in you*
> *will complete it until the day of Jesus Christ."*
> *(Philippians 1:6 KJV)*

I realized at that moment, my friend had just shared with me an actual promise from the Lord. I knew Tommy was going to be alright. Marriage forms a covenant bond between the husband and the wife, which makes the two, one. Since Tommy and I are one through our marriage covenant, I knew the Lord was speaking to Tommy as well.

The reason my faith was so strong was in part because I was raised in a wonderful pastor's home. I was privileged to have a father who lived everything he preached from behind the pulpit. I remember getting up at night and seeing my father in the living room, kneeling by the couch, praying and reading the Bible. He taught me how important it was to read the Bible and believe its words. This caused my faith to grow. The Word of God is very powerful, and it will never return void.

The scripture says,

> "Train up a child in the way he should go:
> and when he is old, he will not depart from it"
> (Proverbs 22:6 KJV)

Trouble comes to every man, every woman, and to every family from time to time. Troublesome times are seasonal for everyone. When we place our confidence in God, He will tell us what to do and He will carry us.

> "Cast all your anxiety on Him,
> because He cares (will take care) of you."
> (1 Peter 5:7 Amplified)

That is exactly what I did; I trusted in Him. Jesus is a miracle worker, and I *knew* it. I remembered as a child while I was very sick with a horrible earache, the people of God prayed for me and I was completely healed. I also remember while at Bible

College, I was in a serious car wreck and the doctor said I had a very severe concussion. I was sitting in a chair in the lobby of the college and not really feeling well at all. I sat there battling with a concussion and when Tommy walked by, he laid his hands on my head, prayed for me and within twenty minutes, the Lord had completely healed me. I knew by experience the Lord was going to bring my husband out of this awful calamity that had come upon him.

> *Though the emotions were heavy around me, I felt the presence of the Lord still bringing peace. My heart did not have the shouting or dancing kind of peace, but more of a sweet aroma of His love and comfort.*

My experience of being raised in a household of faith (of knowing that scripture talks of the many miracles Jesus did, of receiving healing from God personally, of seeing God move so many times in my personal life and throughout ministry) all contributed to my belief that God can, and does, do miracles. All this had built my faith, so I could trust God now that everything was going to be alright with Tommy.

Eventually, the nurse came and took me to see him. They allowed those that were with me to see him as well. The hallway was very long we had to walk down (but it probably was not as long as it felt), then we turned a corner and two doors opened.

When we went through these doors, we were in the nurses' station. There were rooms in front of the nurses' desk that formed a square pattern. The rooms had sliding glass doors, some patients were in them.

As we walked into Tommy's room, the light was very dim. I saw a monitor with his vital signs on it and an IV in his arm. I was so grateful he was asleep. He would not be happy knowing that an IV was stuck in his arm.

At that moment, all I could do was sit next to him and quietly pray. I was not praying like so many others would think. I was not praying a prayer in the spirit of desperation and grief, but in assurance, knowing God was hearing my prayer.

When I went before God, I honored the Lord for who He

was. I worshiped Him, knowing He was there and His presence was there. So, the praying I did was not in pleading, but rather, in confidence knowing the miracle working, creator of all things had this under His control. I just knew He did.

It was a difficult time just watching him lying in the bed, sound asleep. I kept trusting the Lord. Even though he looked so peaceful, but I knew something was not normal. To this day, I cannot explain what I saw, but I just knew it was different than when he slept at night. I have wondered many times if it was the unsettledness of his spirit, but it was soon to be revealed in time what was happening. So, I just stood there, by his bed, holding his hand. I was not about to let go!

Todd stayed with me and explained everything that was going on and what would happen throughout the night. I am grateful that he and Kristie were there with me through it all. Their explanations helped relieve my nerves from so much stress. God is so sweet to send people like them to help us when the enemy hits us so hard. No matter what, our faith must stay active. Never stop believing, trusting, and knowing He alone is our healer.

As we headed back to the waiting room, I leaned over the railing and placed a kiss on his face. I slowly lowered myself down in a nearby chair, and at that moment I felt as if I was living someone else's life.

Though the emotions were heavy around me, I felt the presence of the Lord still bringing peace. It was not the shouting or dancing kind of peace, but in my heart it was more of a sweet aroma of His love and comfort. I felt His arms wrap around me. I was experiencing an inner peace that I could not really explain. As stated earlier it was a peace that surpasses all the understanding of the mind of man.

> *"And the peace of God, which transcends all understanding, will guard your hearts and your minds in Christ Jesus."*
> *(Philippians 4:7 Amplified)*

At 12:30 a.m. Thursday morning, one by one, everyone began to leave and go home. One of my assistants, at the time, stayed with me and helped me turn one of the chairs, into a bed. She stayed through the night with me in case I needed help. As I laid there on my make-shift bed, with a pillow and blanket, I was thinking to myself, finally our church was going in a direction we had asked of the Lord, but now we are dealing with this. I never thought in a million years, I would be with my husband at the hospital with a bleed on his brain.

> *I took his hand and as I waited, I prayed. I did not feel the need to beg, but I just talked to the Lord as if He was sitting in the room with Tommy and me. I thanked the Lord for what He can do and who He is.*

I laid in the presence of the almighty God of Heaven and earth, the great Jehovah, my Healer, the Peace Giver and the Lover of my soul. I never questioned Him, I trusted Him. I think about that moment every now and then of how my mind and my heart continued reaching with hope and understanding.

I kept thinking to myself, *this feeling cannot be normal. It has to be the Spirit of God on the inside of me taking me to a place where I can stand strong, solely on the Word of God.*

If you are a Christian, the Spirit of God lives inside of you, so let Him guide you through the storm. Trust Him that He would never leave you. The Spirit of God wants to direct and lead us when we are under attack and especially when we battle with weaknesses. This is why you need the Spirit of God with you. Let Him overtake you when you are "slapped in the face" by the devil.

Our reaction in times of trouble can and should be words of hope and thoughts of peace. It is times like these when your mind wants to doubt, but you know to walk in faith you cannot allow yourself to worry or fret. He will bring you out of the storm. He did it for us, He will do it for you. Around 2:00 a.m., I checked on Tommy. They told me, "You are not allowed to come in here until 6:00 a.m.;" visiting hours were every three hours. I had to wait every three hour intervals to see Tommy. They would not allow anyone to visit him throughout the night. However, by the grace of God, the nurse would sneak me into

Tommy's room for the night. I sat there by his side, looking out the sliding glass door with his curtain half pulled, watching the nurses.

I took his hand and as I waited, I prayed. I thanked the Lord for what He can do and who He was. I purposely took this time to honor Him and praise Him for all the past things He had already done for me and my husband. I mean, without God, we would not have anything. God had been so good to Tommy and me. I had to praise Him. You must learn, when you are in trouble, praise will change things every time. Worship will shift your heart and change the atmosphere into sweet peace. It will give you the strength you need to ignore the fear trying to fight you. It will cause you to pay close attention to the Lord when He is trying to talk to you. It will put you in a more sensitive place where you can see His promises come to pass in your lifetime. Trust me, it works. Remember: *never, ever bite the hand that feeds you*, even when it is Jesus.

Around 3:30 am, I walked back to the waiting room to lie down. I drifted off to sleep again, and deep inside of me I knew, *all was still well.*

I woke up to go back into Tommy's room at 6:00 am. As one of my assistants and I walked into his room, He was still in a medically induced sleep. The window in his room was so large it covered the entire wall of the room. It was so dark the night before, I had not even realized how large the window was. As the sun shined on my back, I sat facing the sliding glass door watching the nurses moving around.

Then people started coming in to see their loved ones down the hallway. We sat waiting for the report of how well Tommy was doing, so we could go home that day or hopefully at least the next. I just knew we would soon be going home with a sweet testimony to share with everyone with whom we would come in contact. His room was quiet and very peaceful. I did not think of anything but leaving soon.

Finally, around 11:00 am, the nurse came in to check his vitals and his eyes. I learned a lot of things while being there and one of those important ones was checking the eyes. It tells you what the brain is doing. The eyes will show if there is a problem with pressure in the brain. So after checking Tommy's vitals, she walked out of the room about ten feet and turned around and came back in. She looked at his eyes again and said she would be right back. I did not know what was going on.

The next thing I saw was a large machine of some kind being pushed down the hall toward me. Following this, Tommy's nurse asked me to step out into the hall with her.

She began to explain, "Tommy needs to have brain surgery immediately or he could die!"

Boy, was I not expecting this!

Chapter 5

God Blocked It

Karen

The nurse was very nervous and shaky. Even after seeing her reaction, I still felt so much peace. I was a little anxious, but not fearful. It is hard to explain the feeling I had. I did not like what I felt, and at the same time, I knew God was in control.

She told us, "I have called the brain surgeon and he is on his way." "They will be putting Tommy into a deeper sleep so they can intubate him. They are about to prepare him for surgery."

I felt like a whirlwind was around me. Tommy was going to have BRAIN SURGERY?!! I was just numb and at the same time, I still was not fearful. I actually became concerned about the nurse because she was very upset.

I asked her, "Are you okay? It is going to be okay."

She said, "Yes, this is just very serious."

I still did not budge in my feelings that ALL WAS WELL.

They told us the doctor was twenty minutes away. I do not know how it happened, but the doctor's twenty-minute trip turned into ten minutes. The next thing I knew, I was standing in the hall with our son, Joshuia, Pastor Todd and Kristie along with our family speaking to the doctor. He was very concerned.

After the doctor arrive, Dr. Tomkins, he explained they would try to surgically remove the blood clot that had formed on the brain from the bleed. He said the clot was so large it was pushing on the brain and would eventually kill him. We were told also the procedure would take at least six hours.

At this point, everything began to speed up. They took me down the hall to an elevator. As we went, they started shoving papers in front of me to sign, allowing Tommy to have all the procedures done. I felt as if I entered into a whirlwind again. Not being able to think, I just did what I was told.

I was definitely grateful I did not have to be alone. I thank God for Pastor Todd and Kristie who were there to explain every detail that was happening. Always keep in mind, God really does love us and He is always faithful to give us just what we need.

The Clinards explained to me the doctors would have to do a procedure before the actual brain surgery. This procedure would be to install a PICC line into the vein. This is a peripherally inserted central catheter line, which is a thin tube that goes into your body through a vein. The end of this catheter goes into a large vein near your heart.

Tommy was about to receive a lot of medication which could be very hard on the veins. This procedure would keep this from happening and it would take forty-five minutes to an hour just for that one procedure alone.

After the procedure to install the PICC and before the brain surgery, the Lord allowed me to meet the anesthesiologist who would be monitoring Tommy through brain surgery. He himself had had brain surgery just two years prior. I thought to myself, only God could set this up. I felt at ease knowing he himself had had brain surgery and came out of it and was doing well. What a promise standing in front of me. It gave me even more hope.

God always knows what we need and when we need it. I know the Lord brought him into our dilemma to remind me once again that Tommy was going to be okay.

The brain surgery began at 11:45 a.m. that Thursday, February 22. Several friends and family showed up and the waiting room was packed. We all waited and waited. I could not believe we were waiting for my husband to have brain surgery.

I began to talk to the Lord once again. He was so sweet to my heart, because I could feel Him all around me. Even though the room was full of people waiting to hear the report about Tommy, I felt as though I was in a bubble. It was as if I was being protected by some unseen dome. I could feel God all around me; He was with me every step of the way. It was like someone had laid a warm blanket on me to shield me from any harm.

At 3:00 p.m., I received a call that the surgery was over, and Dr. Tomkins would be down to talk to me as soon as possible. I finally exhaled. I was so glad it did not take six hours for the surgery, as they had initially thought. I could not wait to hear what the doctor had to say.

When the doctor came to speak with me, we all gathered around to hear the report. I think, at that point, everyone was waiting on "pins and needles." Doctor Tomkins met with us and shared that Tommy was doing very well and he was pleased with how the surgery went. I shared with him that we had been praying, and He said to me, "Well keep praying, because whoever you prayed to, works." I grinned and told him, "He really does, and His name is Jesus."

> *I knew he would not like the fact they had completely shaved his head, but I did not care. He was alive and everything was going to be alright.*

He told me Tommy would be brought back up to the CCU in a little while, and I would be able to see him soon. He said, he wanted to keep Tommy asleep for a few days in order for him to recover. This would help the brain rest so it would not have to work so hard to operate the body during recovery. They would also keep him intubated so his brain could rest from breathing and the machine could do it for him.

Later, one of the nurses involved in the surgery procedure told us, after they opened Tommy up, the blood shot across the room! They told me that this is unheard of and actually scared the doctor. He quickly turned Tommy over during surgery to check his eyes and his vital signs. He discovered the pressure on Tommy's brain was completely gone. His eyes and vitals were normal. The doctor was amazed, and he said, "This definitely helped save Tommy's life." We know this was nothing but the hand of God. Is God not amazing?!

Within an hour after returning to the CCU waiting room, I received a phone call from the nurse saying I could go back and see Tommy. I was so excited to be able to see him.

As the doors opened to the CCU, I walk around the nurses' desk and back into the same room as before surgery. I could see the breathing tube in his mouth, which was there to give his brain a few days of rest to heal from the traumatic surgery. They said he would definitely be asleep for about three days. I was so happy to see him! I quickly squeezed his hand to tell him I loved him and I was there for him.

I knew he would not like the fact they had completely shaved his head, but I did not care. He was alive and everything was going to be alright. They had made a large incision in the shape of a horseshoe on the back left of his head, which was closed with staples. Even though he had gone through this type of surgery, he looked so peaceful.

I looked up to see over his head and there lined several bottles and medicines running into an IV, just as before. Soon after I spent some time with Tommy, I thanked the Lord for His goodness and His mercy, and I headed back to the waiting room again.

During this time, we had so many visitors. One by one, they would go into his room and pray for him. Our minister friends from all over the country came again to pray for Tommy. We all gathered together for prayer and waited in faith. The hospital was so kind that they even brought more blankets and pillows to help.

So as we were making ourselves even more comfortable, I looked up to see walking toward me another wonderful man and woman of God who meant the world to me; it was my parents, Pastor Bill and Velda Heaston. At that moment, an even greater peace came over me. Here was the man who taught me how to stand on the Word of God and trust the Lord with my entire heart. I now had the two people who taught me how to stand when the enemy attacks, standing right next to me. I cannot express how much I felt encouraged even the more.

Kristie told me she received a phone call from a friend of ours in Florida, Hilary Hathaway. She told me she, too, had been in prayer and that the Lord had spoken to her as well. She said, the Lord told her to tell me, "I have begun a good work in you, and I will finish that which I have started."

After hearing this, I was so excited I could have shouted right then and there. The Lord gave me confirmation to my promise. She had shared the same thing the pastor's wife had shared with me earlier and neither one of them knew the other. I knew God had spoken. What a confirmation. *I knew I had heard from the Lord!* Tommy was going to be completely healed. Within twenty-four hours, the Lord had spoken the same thing twice, and I stood on it. I got my promise from God and I was excited! When you stand on a promise He has given you, believe that word with your heart and you will receive those things for which you are asking.

"This is the third time I am coming to you. In the mouth of two or three witnesses shall every word be established."
(2 Corinthians 13:1 KJV)

"And whatever you ask in my name, that I will do, that the Father may be glorified in the Son. If you ask anything in my name, I will do it."
(John 14:13-14 KJV)

Also, while we were in the CCU waiting room, we shared how wonderful Jesus is and prayed with so many who were waiting for their loved ones to recover as well. We thought, we might as well minister to those around us. Why not? They need a miracle, too. God is big enough to meet every need.

So, I would go back and forth from Tommy's room to the waiting room. There were so many wanting to see him that we all had to take turns.

It was a very long day, and as the day went on, everyone began returning to their homes. I turned the chair in the waiting room into a bed once again. However, before I settled in for that night, I went to see Tommy one more time. As I came back into the waiting room, I laid down. I was comforted and excited that after all we went through, not only did God talk to me, but He brought the confirmation I needed. I knew Tommy was going to be okay.

On Friday, February 23, 2007, I was ready to be with Tommy. By 6:00 am, I went into his room and it was so peaceful. The doctor came in and shared he was not sure what Tommy would be able to do when he wakes up, so be prepared. He was very concerned, and he told us it was possible Tommy might never preach, sing, walk, talk, or play the organ or keyboard ever again. He told me he would more than likely be a vegetable. He was not sure if Tommy would ever be normal again.

For a split second, I wondered if they had removed part of his brain by accident, then immediately I said to myself, "No, he will be fine."

One of the most important things you must do when you believe for a miracle is you must take every thought captive and make sure it agrees with what the Lord says (II Corinthians 10:4-5). Be sure your thoughts line up with the Word of God, which is the same as His will. You must keep yourself guarded. It is easy to let your thoughts run rampant during these times.

We build our faith in God when we take the time to read the Word. You must learn that what you allow yourself to think about will impact your faith and your emotions. So, control your *thoughts*. This will help you take charge of your feelings and believe in God.

"[Inasmuch as we] refute arguments and theories and reasoning's and every proud and lofty thing that sets itself up against the [true] knowledge of God; and we lead every thought and purpose away captive into the

obedience of Christ (the Messiah, the Anointed One)."

(2 Corinthians 10:5 Amplified)

It was not long before the word got out and more and more ministers, family and friends continued to visit. Together, we were believing for a total miracle, and we all knew in our hearts that God was capable of healing him completely. Together, we were standing on the Word of God.

You see, I wanted to create an atmosphere for a miracle, so I brought in some worship music to play very quietly in his room. I wanted Tommy to feel the presence of the Lord. Even though he was asleep, I knew his spirit was wide awake. I continued to play worship music in his room so the presence of God would bring peace there and would overtake the atmosphere of the hospital.

One of our closest friends, Pastor Jody Rogers, had come into the room. He was standing next to me and he picked up his phone and took a picture.

He explained, "We should take pictures so you can show the miracle." That comment had such an impact on me. I started taking pictures from that day on.

We needed to show the miracle. We needed to have the proof of what was happening, because Tommy was coming out of this valley. If I had not taken pictures, Tommy would never have been able to see what all God had done. He does not remember much of anything from the hospital experience, but the photos helped his memory and the story.

As Pastor Jody and I stood there, we talked about what all we knew God was going to do. Then, the atmosphere shifted. We both felt a different kind of spirit rush into Tommy's room. Even with worship music playing, something had changed, and not for the better. We knew it was the spirit of death.

At the end of Tommy's bed against the wall, was a tall trash can. All of a sudden, the trash can began to shake and immediately Jody and I began to pray and take authority over that spirit. Instantly, that spirit left. We looked at each other in shock. We did not expect that attack, but we were so grateful we were both there. I knew this was no coincidence. I am so thankful for the blood of Jesus which gives you the power and authority over what the enemy would try to do.

God always has a perfect will, just as He has a perfect timing. He will order your footsteps to be at the right place at the right time. I really believe we did not just *happen* to be in the room at that time, but it was God ordained. Trust God when believing for a miracle. Know that He is in charge and He has you.

>
> *The steps of a good man are ordered*
> *by the Lord: and he delights in his way.*
> *(Psalms 37:23 Amplified)*

When we left his room, it had become peaceful again. I thank the Lord for His presence being so real.

Chapter 6

A Fork In The Road

Tommy

My! Our whole life drastically changed overnight. I lived to play the Hammond organ, sing gospel music, and preach. With one sweeping moment, it was all at risk. The doctors said if I made it out alive, I would never play music or preach again. I would only sit in a chair without the ability to understand or speak anything sensible.

I made my choice to follow Jesus when I was a child. I have

had my share of troubles and trials, but to know Jesus is more than a figure in a religious book is worth more than all the money in the world. To put it frankly, if the unbeliever is right, we all have nothing to be concerned about; however, if the Bible is right, then all unbelievers should turn their heart toward a loving God who paid for our salvation with His own life.

This loving God has kept me through every trial that has come my way. The tragic event that overtook my family and me could have sent us hurtling down an unbelieving pathway, changing our hearts concerning God and His Word, but He has seen me through battles and crises too often for me and my family to walk away now. When I made Jesus my choice, it was for better or for worse.

This time was the most difficult of all, but I would not give up on Him then, and I will not give up on Him now.

Like so many others, I have heard my whole life about the story of Heaven. It is a place where the righteous in Christ go when they pass away. I grew up in church, sitting with my family in a pew as we sang songs of that wonderful Heaven so fair, like "When We All Get to Heaven," "Sweeping Through the Gates," and "Everybody Will Be Happy Over There." After a few songs and the announcements, the pastor would stand behind the pulpit, preaching sermons of Heaven and why I should want to go there.

But, although Karen and I both trusted and believed we would spend an eternity in that wonderful place, I know I am blessed that my wife faithfully believed in the promises God gave her: that I would be fine, that she was able to use the authority Jesus gave her over the enemy, trusting Him and having faith in what He says is more important than believing what she saw.

Chapter 7

Faith Was In Charge

Karen

As we had done previously on so many day, Saturday February 24, 2007, was the same. We spent the entire day going back and forth visiting Tommy and praying and talking with others in the waiting room. The doctor came to tell me they were going to wake Tommy the next morning. I was excited to hear such great news. Finally, I was going to get to watch a miracle with my own eyes, hear with my own ears; him talking again to me! We sang and laughed, because we knew that the promise was ours. Family and friends continued to pile into his room.

While waiting, I kept hearing "Code Red" over the hospital system quite a bit. I got tired of hearing "Code Red," so I stood up in the waiting room, put my arms out in the air and commanded the death angel not to return as long as we were in the building. I rebuked the spirit of death! Do you know, the hospital workers in CCU reported this was the first time there had not been a death in weeks? In fact, after this, there was not another Code Red until we left the hospital. God is so faithful.

"For we do not wrestle against flesh and blood, but against principalities, against power, against the rulers of the darkness of this age, against spiritual hosts of wickedness in the heavenly places."
(Ephesians 6:12 KJV)

That evening, I was alone in the CCU waiting room. I stood up and I saw a vision of myself standing in Tommy's shoes. I knew this was the Lord reminding me Tommy and I have a covenant together that makes us one. I said to the Lord, "Tommy and I are one, and if we are one, then I am standing in his shoes and you will see me as Tommy." I could literally see my legs in Tommy's legs, my feet in his shoes.

> *The gift of faith covered me like a warm blanket. It was not a common faith, but a faith only given by God.*

I asked the Lord, "After all the years I have loved you, sold out to you, and honored you, would you honor me/Tommy and completely heal me/Tommy?"

At this moment, I felt the hand of the Lord come and hover over me. I had complete confidence that the healer, Jesus was going to move for us. I knew again Tommy was going to be alright.

I stayed with him as much as they would let me. There were

times they would sneak me in to sit with him and hold his hand. I loved it, because this would allow me the opportunity to quietly pray next to him. I would talk to the Lord and just worship Him. I knew His love outweighed my own for Tommy. I trusted the love that Jesus has for us over any thought or evil imagination. In fact, not even once, did I have the desire to question God with the, "what ifs?"

Casting down imaginations,
and every high thing that exalts itself against
the knowledge of God, and bringing into
captivity every thought to the obedience of Christ;
(2 Corinthians 10:5 Amplified).

I kept my mind on Jesus and His goodness.

The gift of faith covered me like a warm blanket. It was not a common faith, but a faith only given by God. It brings determination and the strength to just stand. It gave me an assurance inside that caused me to not waver or move. I controlled my thoughts. I controlled my emotions. I kept my mind knowing that God was the healer. Faith was in charge.

At this point, I had stayed at the hospital for almost 13 days, and I needed to go home to gather some things for myself and Tommy. I needed to pick up some fresh clothes for Tommy to wear back home. While this was a warranted trip, I did not want to leave Tommy. I did not want to miss out on anything that could happen or change. At any given moment, I was always expecting Tommy to sit up and be completely healed.

On Saturday, February 24, after everyone insisting I should go get some rest in an actual bed, I left and went to Pastor Todd and Kristie's house to get some sleep. The only thing my mind kept telling me was, I cannot wait, in the morning Tommy was going to wake up.

Chapter 8

The Shift

Karen

Sunday, February 25, at 6:00 a.m., Todd and I left their home to go back to the hospital. I wanted to be there when they woke Tommy out of the drug-induced sleep he had been in since the evening of Wednesday, February 21. This would mean he would finally be breathing on his own and we would be closer to going home to tell our miracle to everyone. This was an exciting day of victory!

We arrived in time, and soon after we were notified that Tommy was breathing on his own. After a few hours of breathing on his own, he began to stir. He was waking up! The staples they put in the back of the head must have started bothering him, because Tommy would reach up to try to pull at them. I tried to stop him from putting his hand on his head and he finally responded to me. I quickly told the nurse, "He just spoke to me. *He spoke!*" I think my heart leaped within me at that moment.

This day was such a wonderful day. He woke up and saw so many of our friends and family who had come to see him. The air was filled with happiness, the storm was about to be over!

That evening the nurse came in and asked Tommy a few questions. She first asked, "Do you know who the president is?"

Tommy said, "Me." He was so funny. The real "*him*" was there. His body was very weak, but Tommy was awake. I noticed his body was in recovery and healing from the trauma it had been through, but his spirit was well aware of his surroundings. I saw for the first time the difference between the body and the spirit of man/woman.

> *"The strong spirit of a man*
> *sustains Him in bodily pain or trouble,*
> *but a weak and broken spirit who can*
> *raise up and bear?"*
> *(Proverbs 18:14. Amplified)*

This means, when we are weak in body, our spirit becomes strong, but only if our spirit is full of Jesus. Only if you have allowed Him to rule in your life and you have a relationship with Him. If so, your spirit will rise to the occasion at hand. The world might call this "survival mode," but it is something more; for even those who do not have a relationship with Jesus can be in survival mode. This is being able to utilize a strength that is more than your own.

The nurses tried again to speak to Tommy by calling his name. This time, he did *not* respond! It was as if he did not know who Tommy was. Once she presented him with a question, he quickly answered with great humor. He was very witty. He would say the funniest things.

The nurse continued to ask him questions like, "Do you know where you are?"

Tommy responded, "I am at Colter's Bar-B-Q."

Well, she thought that Tommy was not thinking correctly, but I knew he was. I knew he was playing with her.

They asked, "Can you see how many fingers I am holding up?"

Tommy would not answer her.

I saw that the nurse was becoming concerned, but I knew Tommy was playing. I had to find a way to let her know he really could see her fingers. When Tommy was young his mother played a game with him called, "bum bum beat the drum." You would take your fist and gently beat the back of the person in front of you. Then while tapping, you would say "bum bum beat the drum, how many fingers do I hold up?" Then that person would have to guess how many fingers you were holding up behind their back. After playing this with Tommy, it was revealed how he was thinking. This proved to be okay and his vision was good. IT WORKED! She could not believe it. Tommy began to laugh. He was playing with us the whole time.

Tommy would talk to people, but not open his eyes very much—just a squint at times and then not at all. He told me later, he remembered seeing me and another person when they came to see him. He said we looked very distorted, as if he had triple vision. He said no one looked normal at all. So, to avoid the unclear vision, he would keep his eyes closed.

There was a missionary from Mexico who heard about Tommy. The man called and said he was in Texas and asked if he could come and pray for Tommy. Although I did not know him personally, I felt it was the Lord. When he arrived, I took him back to see Tommy. While he was there, along with Jody Rogers, my father and I took communion with Tommy.

When times are hard dealing with sickness and diseases, we should always remember the covenant God made with man is extremely important. We had to continue to stand on the healing promise God gave in His Word in Isaiah 53:5, *"He (Jesus) was wounded (suffering injury or bodily harm) for our transgressions (violation of God's law, sin), He was bruised (injured by striking without breaking skin) for our iniquities (the act of our sin), the chastisement (a corporal punishment; a beating for our peace was placed upon Him and by His stripes, WE ARE HEALED! (to make whole; restore to health)."* Nothing missing, nothing broken. I felt the Lord the whole time as we stood there and talked about the Lord. The missionary prayed for Tommy's healing and recovery, then left.

I am so grateful to all who stood faithfully in the gap to pray and give. They took time out from their busy schedules to come pray for Tommy as well as me, and our son Joshuia. They are all part of this great miracle. I thank God for each of them.

*"And when he had given thanks,
he brake it, and said, Take, eat: this is my body,
which is broken for you: this do in
remembrance of me. After the same manner
also he took the cup, when he had supped, saying, this cup is
the new testament in my blood: this do ye,
as oft as ye drink it, in remembrance of me."*

(1Corinthian 11:24-25 NKJV)

God is very strategic in sending those He has chosen to pray. Prayer changes things and it is important we keep prayer at the center part of our lives. Nothing will change without it.

Monday, February 26, they moved Tommy to a lower level ICU. The room was like any other hospital room. It had a bed, a night stand, and a television. Next to the bed was a chair that lay out into a bed. It was not the best thing to sleep on, but I was not about to leave him. I was so glad to be close to him.

After entering his new room, he told us he did not like the atmosphere of his room. He was asked where he would like to go. Tommy said, "The Anatole would be nice." (The Anatole Hotel is a very popular, five-star hotel in Dallas.)

I learned something I would love to teach you. When you are that sick, the spirit takes over. It is not that he just disliked the colors of the room or what it looked like, but he did not like the atmosphere. He did not like how the room felt because of the spiritual atmosphere that existed inside that room.

I did not realize at the time, but there have been many times since looking back, where I wished I would have stopped everything, gone into that room, and prayed that the peace of

God and His anointing would be in the room.

No matter where we traveled, we would always pray blessings over every hotel room or house in which we stayed. During this time, I was so focused on caring for Tommy that I did not think to pray over his room before taking residence.

The nurses were still trying to get Tommy to answer them by calling his name. He still would not respond to them. Pastor Todd suggested to the nurses to say his name as Pastor instead of using the name Tommy, and it worked!

I thought it was amazing how he would only answer to the title of the "office" God gave him to work in. It makes sense. The real "him" was his spirit and that is what was alive. The spirit inside of you is the real you. Since his spirit was strong, and his flesh was weak, he would only respond to what his spirit connected to. And for him, that was the office of Pastor.

That same night at 7:00 p. m., I turned on a worship CD and I was going to pray with Tommy. One of the members of the ministry was there and joined us in prayer.

As we worshipped, the Spirit of God walked into that room and the atmosphere completely changed. We forgot where we were; the anointing was so strong. The Lord was so sweet. When you apply the scriptures from the Bible to your prayers, the devil must step back. He has to back down!

> *"For where two or three are gathered together in my name, there am I in the midst of them."*
> (Matthew 18:20 KJV)

The Word of God is true. We began to pray and agree for the same thing in unity. There were three of us agreeing; worshiping and honoring the Lord. Tommy would lift his hands and begin to pray *very loudly*. No one came in the room during this time. Each night from 7:00 a.m. - 9:00 p.m., no one disturbed us at all. I am not sure if they were afraid, because of *what* they heard, but they did not disturb us at all.

It was so wonderful to have that time in the presence of the Lord and to be alone with Him. There were three people in that room praying that night, but I only felt God!

"And though a man might prevail
against him who is alone, two will withstand him.
A threefold cord is not quickly broken."
(Ecclesiastes 4:12 KJV)

Chapter 9

Anew

Karen

Tuesday, February 27, 2007, they began therapy with Tommy. He had to relearn everything: to sit, stand, walk, bend over, pick up things...literally, everything.

The next morning, the occupational therapist came into his room to begin teaching him his first exercise of sitting and how to sit up straight. When he attempted to sit up, he started leaning too far to the left. They would touch his right shoulder to tell him he was leaning too far, so he would lean back to the right. Now he began to lean too far to the right. So, they would touch the left shoulder to let him know he was leaning too far. This exercise helped him understand how to sit up straight. Within just a few tries, he was able to sit up on his own.

It amazed me that he did not remember how to sit up but understood every instruction they gave him. It is amazing how God has made us; *He* is amazing!

That afternoon they came back into his room for therapy to teach him how to stand on his own. They helped him learn how to push himself up from a sitting position to standing upright. The next step was, once he was in a standing position, to be able to sit himself in a wheelchair, and the chair next to the bed. He was not able to walk very well but sitting in the chair was such a great accomplishment!

Tommy has been very independent and has had a determined nature most of his life, so you can only imagine the difficulties he faced having to need this kind of assistance. He wrestled with his emotions, being a very private person, now having to have people help him.

To find out where he was in the healing process, they would ask Tommy where he was. Every time they used the title "Pastor," he would answer, "At the hospital."

Then they would ask him, "Do you know why you are here?"

He would tell them, "Well, I am having a hospital situation."

When the doctor came in and asked how Tommy was doing, I shared with him that he had been singing. Tommy would sing over and over again an old church song, "When I See the Blood, I will pass over you."

The doctor asked, "What kind of song is he singing?"

I said, "He is singing a church song."

He asked, "Does it make any sense?"

With a puzzled look, I told him, "Of course it does."

The doctor was baffled. He told me, those songs should not have made any sense. Given what he had just been through, Tommy's cognitive skills should not have been that good at all. The doctor then shared Tommy's vision, more than likely, would not be normal at all. He was not sure if both eyes would struggle seeing but thought the right eye would definitely be affected.

I trusted the Lord and believe he would see as he needed. I knew God was creating this miracle and all I had to do was believe. So, as I did my part, God did His.

That afternoon, the nurses came back in to help Tommy with his therapy and exercising skills. We repeated all of his movements again and again. If we had not moved him consistently, he would have never walked again on his own. For some time, his mobility exercise was to get into a wheelchair. Even though he hated it, he had to endure it if he was ever going to walk on his own again.

So, eventually, he was able to get into a wheelchair. Boy, I was so excited inside. I knew we were getting closer and closer to our promise. I was tickled to see the miracle of God taking place before my very eyes. Miracles were happening all around us. Some were so small, if

Each night the Spirit of God would move very heavily, and Tommy would weep and pray in the spirit.

we did not realize it, we would have missed the lesson and the tiniest miracles God was giving to us.

I think we overlook some very important miracles every day of our lives. We become so busy these days, we do not even see them. Miracles like being able to lean over in your own strength and kiss someone you dearly love, like driving yourself to the store and taking care of your own personal hygiene. We have learned to not only appreciate the big things, but the tiniest things as well. Thank you, Jesus!

Every day Tommy had a lot of visitors coming and going. The spirit on the inside of him was so alive. He would prophesy over many of them who came to check on his progress. All the while his body had been mending, his spirit had been depending on the Lord's presence. His spirit was strong, and at the very same time, his flesh was weak. Very weak. In Matthew 26:41, Jesus told Peter to watch and pray so that he would not fall into temptation. Your spirit is willing, but your flesh is weak. The gift God has given is always alive within each person.

> *"To another the working of miracles;*
> *to another prophecy; to another discerning of spirits;*
> *to another divers kinds of tongues; to another the*
> *interpretation of tongues:"*
> *(1 Corinthians 12:10 KJV)*

Finally the day came and they moved Tommy from the wheelchair to a regular chair that set next to his bed. Unbelievable, it had not even been a week since the brain surgery when I was told he may not talk, sit, stand, walk or be normal again. But he had graduated from sitting in a wheelchair to a regular chair already.

Again, every evening at 7:00 p.m., I turned on a CD to worship and pray. Tommy and I prayed and worshipped. The Spirit of the Lord walked in the room as before and the atmosphere completely shifted. God's presence filled the room like an invisible cloud. We would forget where we were.

At times the Lord's anointing can almost feel tangible. If God is really real, and I know He is, His glory should be felt when you praise Him for His goodness. Many times, Tommy would begin to speak of the things the Lord was showing him, and it was incredibly powerful!

At the end of our prayer time I asked him where he was, and he would say, "We're in the Upper Room." The Upper Room refers to the day of Pentecost where the Holy Spirit filled the whole house where the disciples were gathered to pray, Acts 2:4. They saw with tongues of fire that separated and came to rest on each of them. All of them were filled with the Holy Spirit and began to speak in other tongues as the Spirit enabled them. To read more about it, I recommend you refer to the Book of Acts, chapters 1 and 2.

"And they were all filled with the Holy Spirit and began to speak with other tongues, as the Spirit gave them utterance."
(Acts 2:4 NKJV)

He continued to boldly say, "We are here in His presence."

The presence of God was SO STRONG that he could only compare it to the knowledge he had from the Bible that tells of the miracle that happened in *the Upper Room*. Each night, the Spirit of God would move very heavily, and Tommy would weep and pray in the spirit.

One night, in a weeping voice, Tommy told those who were standing by his bed, "Go get the wheat!" "Go get the wheat!" "Time is running out!" "Time is running short." "Be careful as you gather the wheat and do not step on them." "There are baskets of wheat that need to be distributed." "Be sure and follow through." "Make sure we captivate the anointing!" "Get ready!" "Don't miss anything and get it all."

I could tell he had been weeping as he told me in a desperate tone, "I cannot get it all, I cannot get it all." As he kept on repeating, we assured him we would help him, and he would be able to get all the wheat. That seemed to bring him relief and finally he drifted off to sleep. He was so troubled about the wheat. He told me later the Spirit of God told him that Christians would miss harvest time for souls that are lost and their purpose for living would be in vain.

This is where I started learning the real difference between the body, the soul, and the spirit, which make up the three parts of the human being. We were all made in the likeness and the image of God for His glory.

God is one, yet He is three, three in one.

Without going into much detail, God created man: spirit, soul and body. The body is the flesh with which we all are covered. The soul of man is where we make our choices and make everyday decisions by using our own will. The spirit of man is the part of us that is reserved for God alone. It is the part of man that never dies, the eternal part. You and I are a three-part being, just like God.

I am sure this is why he struggled when they would call him Tommy, because in the spirit, the Lord had given him a title of an office called Pastor/Evangelist. This is why when the nurses called him Pastor, his spirit responded to them. He knew the Lord had placed that calling on his life. If God called him by that title, then that is who he was.

He could not operate by his physical brain at the time, since he was in the state of healing. His physical was no longer prominent in him. He struggled with his flesh, but Tommy's spirit man was responding to the Spirit of God.

Remember the scripture I shared: "A man's spirit sustains him in sickness" (Proverbs 18:14). His physical man was fighting to regain life while the spirit man was alive and well.

Chapter 10

Prayer Of Obedience

Karen

T he Holy Spirit of God would come into his room each night and we would simply sit in His presence. The peace was like an umbrella hovering over us, as if fear, doubt, and worry did not exist. I remember nurses would even come in and say, "Wow, this room is just so different from all the other rooms! It is so peaceful!"

Wednesday, February 28, Tommy began more intensive

> *Tommy was very honest with people. I would tell visitors, "If you do not want the Lord to reveal things in your life and the truth to be told, do not go in his room."*

therapy. By that time, he had learned quickly to sit and stand all by himself, and with just an assistance of a walker and they would escort him down the hall and around the nurses' station. It did not take much time for him to tire out very quickly, but he continued to push himself to get better. It was so exciting to see the progress.

His visitors came and went daily, and Tommy continued to prophecy to many of them. It was incredible to observe a perfect God moving like that through a man that was so weak in his body. I think of the scripture that says,

"But God chose the foolish things of the world to confound the wise, God chose the weak things of the world to shame the strong!"
(1 Corinthians 1:27 KJV)

I remember specifically one day as my father was sitting next to Tommy's bed. Everyone was talking, moving, laughing, and visiting, but as he sat very quietly, I knew he was praying. I could feel God. I saw a tear run down his face and I knew my dad was petitioning God to move for us. I knew he was asking the Lord to completely heal Tommy. I felt the presence of the Lord through the prayer of this man. I knew with my father praying, something was going to happen.

The nurses continued to exercise Tommy's cognitive skills. Every single day someone would come in to work with him. One particular day a speech therapist came in and Tommy struggled to stay awake. I shared that I felt the medications were keeping him too tired. I told the nurse he was not used to medicine like this.

I explained to her that he/we do not drink alcohol, and asked if she thought the drugs were likely too much for him? They made him feel off, very tired and scattered in his ability to talk. She proceeded to ask, "You mean you have never taken a drink?"

Tommy looked up at her, and answered, "No, never! Do you?"

She said, "Well, did not Jesus turn the water into wine?"

He told her, "You can do better than that!" I thought at that moment, Tommy is here!

Tommy was very honest with people. I would tell visitors, "If you do not want the Lord to reveal things in your life and the truth to be told, do not go in his room." There were a few that refused to come in the room, as they feared of something would be revealed.

That Wednesday night at 7:00 p.m., I put the worship CD on as usual, and the Spirit of God showed up again, and Tommy shared what the Lord was telling him.

I asked, "Where are you?"

He asked, "Physically or spiritually?"

I answered, "Spiritually."

He told me he was making a decree before the Lord. Not knowing what the decree was, I knew it was serious and that whatever he was decreeing to the Lord was very powerful and something powerful was going to happen.

At 10:30 p.m., a woman came in with a pastor friend of ours along with other visitors. The woman had been in a revival and she really felt she needed to pray over Tommy. There were several people there and we all began to pray for the miracle to be done. As we held hands and agreed in prayer, the power of God became even stronger in the room. The presence of the Lord could be felt everywhere. She shared that in the meeting that night Evangelist Kim Clement said there was someone lying in the hospital who had just had brain surgery and God was going to heal him.

At that moment, I knew God had given me another promise to hang on to. It was so sweet that He kept reminding me that our miracle was on the way. See, you must learn to hang on to what you know. You must keep yourself focused on the promise and our promise was, "I have begun a good work in you, and I will finish what I have started." When God says something, He will always complete it. This is why it is so important to have faith and to have a relationship with Jesus.

Chapter 11

The Promise

Karen

It was now Thursday, March 1. Tommy was still working on walking with a walker. The nurses continued to take him down the hall and around the nurses' station. They would ask him every day, "Do you know where you are?" "Do you know who you are?" Up to this point, he had never told them who he was and what hospital he was in.

Instead, he would tell them things like, "Puddin' Tane, ask me again and I will tell you the same." Sometimes he would tell them, he was at the grocery store shopping and there were times he was not sure. There were only two times he told them he was in a hospital, but he was not sure where. He knew who the visitors were when they came in, but he could not tell you who he was. He would minister to nurses and share with the doctors the goodness of God.

At 11:30 p.m. that night, Tommy's head started seeping. The nurses notified the doctor and he came to sew it up. Tommy never felt a thing and he was wide awake. We talked with the doctor while he did the procedure. I was amazed Tommy never felt any of the pain. God is so faithful. We personally know Him as our physician: Jesus, our healer.

It had been a long, but good, week of progress. So much had been accomplished since the surgery. He reached the place where he was able to sit, stand, and walk with a walker.

On March 2, things began to become a little odd, even for us. The therapist worked with Tommy as always. There were more visitors who came to see him. He never struggled with recognizing people before, but today was different. It was as if he did not know anyone. I had to explain to him who each person was, but before this time, he would remember. In fact, he did not even recognize his own son, Joshuia.

It was very strange to me and I could have really begun to be bothered, but again, *"I did not allow myself to go there."* I would *not* let it override my peace and the fact that I *knew!* I did not allow worry to place fear in my heart; yet, at the same time I recognized something was not right.

One of our pastor friends called and said he had been in prayer and the Lord spoke to him about Tommy. He shared how he drove and drove around Dallas, praying the Lord would change the circumstances around us. He did not know what was about to happen, but he told me I was going to receive some very bad news. He told me when I did, I was not to be moved by the news. He told me the Lord said, on the third day, God would raise Tommy up and to know that "the Lord has it in His control."

I told him, I would be ready, while inhaling with a deep breath. In the midst of all we were going through, I could still see God move on our behalf. And I continued to refuse to budge from the promise God gave me, *to trust Him with everything I had.*

Our pastor friend, still feeling unsettled, came in person to the hospital to see Tommy. When he walked in, Tommy instantly knew who he was. All day long Tommy had not known anyone else, but he knew him. This pastor was the only person Tommy recognized. I was so glad I *never* entertained the fear. Not even once!

I am extremely blessed that at a young age, I was taught what the Bible says. Learning who Jesus really is when I was a child really helped me to learn how to trust God. This reminds me that the Bible tells us to raise up a child in the way they should go that they would not depart from it when they grow up. Tommy and I made that a priority as we raised our son, Joshuia.

"Train up a child in the way he should go:
and when he is old, he will not depart from it."
(Proverbs 22:6 KJV)

However, you teach your children, they will not depart from

it. If I had not known how to walk in trust, my heart would have been carried away from me and I would have lost my husband for sure. The foundation of faith I received as a child was solid in this situation as I held on to the arms of God's peace I felt wrapped around me. I kept feeling the presence of God hovering over me, which strengthened my faith. Once again, I *knew!*

The nurse came in later that afternoon and really struggled with Tommy's PICC line. I could see also there was a problem and I shared with her something did not look right. The skin was turning red around it and it did not look good. They were supposed to replace parts of it to keep it clean, to avoid infection, so she took his entire PICC line *completely* out. She was supposed to have it replaced, but she never did.

> *The Spirit came in the room in such a sweet way, as He had every night we had been there. We all began to pray together once again.*

At the end of the day, at 7:00 p.m., I turned our worship music back on, and the Spirit came in the room in such a sweet way, as He had every night. We all began to pray together once again. The scripture, 1 Thessalonians 5:17, *pray without ceasing*, fit our description. We honored the Lord with our worship, but this time it did not last as long as usual. It was different. Tommy was tired and just needed to rest. So, we went to bed earlier than normal that night.

Saturday, March 3, at 5:30 a.m., while lying in the chair-bed next to Tommy's bed, I was awakened by a noise. I reached over and felt inside of his bed with my hand only to find the bed was empty! Tommy was not there! I jumped up! I was startled to find Tommy lying face-down on the hospital floor. I quickly ran to the hallway and yelled for help. Nurses from all over started running from everywhere. They picked him back up and put him in the bed.

They discovered that when he fell out of the bed, he hit his head on the ground which caused a mark on his forehead.

The nurse began to question him. "What is your name?"

Tommy said, "Tommy Drumm."

I was amazed and so excited. Wow! That was the first time he had gotten it right.

The nurse then asked, "Do you know where you are?"

Tommy said, "Yes, Plano Medical Center."

I could not believe what I was hearing. He knew! He knew his name and where he was. I shared with a giggle and excitement, "We should have hit him on the head a long time ago since that hit on the head made him remember everything."

The nurse asked a few more questions and he knew the answers. We settled back down and fell back to sleep. This time I pushed my chair-bed to the other side of his bed, so he would not be able to get out of bed again.

Two hours later, at 7:00 a.m., I woke up to Tommy saying, "Something is wrong. Hey, something is wrong!"

The light in his room was on dim. I could not see very clearly what was going on. When I sat up, I saw something like water on his head and shoulders. I thought, *"Oh no, how in the world did he get water on him?"* When I turned the light on, I was shocked to see it was not water at all!

Chapter 12

The Confirmation

Karen

The back of his head and pillow, all the way down to his shoulders, including the bed, had blood everywhere! The cut where they had closed him from surgery was bleeding profusely, gushing out with every heartbeat. I yelled at the top of my lungs for a nurse and they came running again. They got me a stack of gauze about four inches thick and I held it on the back of his head.

Tommy was bleeding very rapidly. The gauze was filled

within seconds. The nurse kept handing me more and more gauze about 3 inches thick, all at the same time trying to get the doctor on the phone. Tommy's blood was everywhere.

Tommy began to be in violent, excruciating pain! It gripped his body so violently from the top of his head to the bottom of his feet. The bed began to shake. The blood was coming out so fast I was having a hard time keeping up with it. The nurses kept handing me more and more gauze. They kept filling up faster than I could retrieve another clean gauze on this open gap. Together, we kept applying fresh gauze to the eruption to stop the blood.

During this violent shaking from the pain and the blood pouring from his head, he began to cry out, "Read the Word! Read the Word!" I did not have the time to stop what I was doing or the chance to call anyone, but God did. I looked up and unexpectedly, one of our friends walked into the room. I was so glad to see her. I could not believe it. I asked her why she was here, and she said she just felt she needed to come up and check on us.

While I held the gauze in place, I told her to open the Bible and start reading every healing scripture she could find. She started in Genesis and she proceeded to read every Word on healing. Tommy hollered out telling her, "Read another one." So, she would go to the next scripture. He would say again, "Read another one," then again, "Read another one," until she got to the scripture that read,

"Thus says the Lord, the God of your
father David, I have heard your prayer,
I have seen your tears; behold, I will heal you.
On the third day you shall go
up to the house of the Lord."

(2 Kings 20:5 KJV)

When she read that verse, Tommy said, "Read it again!" So, she read it again. He said, "Read it again!" And she did, over and over, until the pain began to leave, and he fell asleep. The bleeding began to lighten up. The bleeding was now very little.

> *Tommy's condition was so critical...but God had already delivered His Word before the problem was executed.*

The Word put him to rest and stopped the bleeding. The Bible is God's living Word; it works! As you read it and through faith activate it, things begin to happen. It certainly did for us that night.

Tommy did not know anything, but the spirit on the inside of him knew the Lord's promise that was given to us the day before, "On the third day he would rise up!" I will always thank God for our Pastor Friend that took the time to pray and hear from the Lord that day. I was sure the Lord was guiding him through this storm even as weak as he was (Prov. 18:14). We received a promise and a confirmation with the Word of God. When God gives us a promise, it will happen. His word is a PROMISE.

He was in so much pain from 7:30 a.m. – 9:30 a.m. When the nurse came into the room and saw Tommy asleep, she became afraid, thinking that he was already gone.

She checked his eyes and said, "He is asleep?"

I said, "Yes."

She said, "What happened?"

I told her, "We read the Word to him and it gave him rest. The Word brings peace."

Not understanding what "the Word" meant, she asked, "What do you mean?"

I told her, "The Bible." She was amazed it put him to sleep.

As we waited for the doctor, we found out Dr. Tomkins, the first brain surgeon, was out of town, so another doctor, Dr. Morgan had to step in.

Dr. Morgan ordered another CT scan at 11:30 a.m. I waited in Tommy's room and my heart was still at peace. I had a promise and I stood on it with all that was in me. I *knew!*

They came running into my room telling me Tommy was headed back to surgery. The nurse told me there was a second bleed in the same place, but now the bleed was much larger than before. Now he was in greater danger. I found myself running down the hall again to sign more papers for them to do what needed to be done to save his life.

By 1:00 p.m. that afternoon, he was headed back to have a second brain surgery. This time it felt different. This time was *so much* more serious than before.

I have to stop with this story for a moment and tell you that this moment, while writing this book, I am listening to the Christian music channel and the same CD we played in the hospital just started playing right now. I believe there are NO coincidences in God. God is always a present help in the time of trouble. I knew He was covering our lives and had Tommy in His divine hands. God will never let us down and I want you to know that - to know it and believe it.

If you know someone, anyone, including yourself, that needs healing – whether it be physical or emotional – he/she/you will receive healing if you will believe God is a healer. Believe what He does for one He can do for another. He is no respecter of persons (Rom. 2:11). That means every single man and woman are created equal. He has an equal and unconditional love for every human being. I am so glad God does not play favorites.

"For there is no respect of persons with God."

(Romans 2:11 KJV)

Some of you will get an instant spontaneous miracle of healing while others will get a progressive healing. I believe that every one of you reading this testimony will receive a miracle and it is coming to your home. There is an old church song that goes like this, *"Only believe. Only believe. All things are possible, only believe."* My advice for you during your test is for you to just believe!

I was headed to the ICU waiting room for the second time and I received word the doctor was very upset, because around 7:30 a.m. that morning the nurse had taken Tommy's PICC line completely out. The devil once again, was trying very hard to kill him. The incompetence or distraction of that nurse was used by the enemy and caused Tommy to have to have another separate procedure before the brain surgery in order to reinsert the PICC line.

Tommy's condition was so critical that they did not want to take the time to do this, but they had no choice. The devil was really pushing him to the edge. He was using anything he could get his hands on to destroy Tommy, but he could not overcome the promise of God. God had already delivered His Word before the problem existed.

Once again we waited. This time was very different, though. Something was not right. There was such an eerie quietness. There were only a few people gathered around this time waiting for the surgery to end. It was not like before with over forty people in the waiting room. This time happened so quickly; I did not have much time to think.

I sat in the waiting room very still. I felt no fear or doubt, and there a deep quiet feeling that everything was going to be okay. So I sat still and refused to allow the enemy in any way to detour everything I was believing God for and every promise on which I was standing.

At 2:30 p.m., the doctor called us to go upstairs to the CCU waiting room. This time no one came out and talked with us. I went straight to the CCU waiting room and waited for what seemed like forever for them to let me go back and see him. During the first surgery I was able to see him within thirty minutes after the surgery. This time was very different from the first surgery.

Finally, at 5:00 p.m., they called me to his room. As I entered, there was a nurse who was very busy and had a very serious air while working with Tommy. The room was a corner shaped room, not as large as the last one, with sliding glass doors. You could see the nurses' station much better.

Hanging above his head there were several bottles and bags pumping his medicine into him. The room felt very different this time. Something was not the same, I could feel such heaviness. There was a nurses' swivel stool I sat on as I watched. I knew by the way the nurse was acting something was not right. I looked up and saw his blood pressure and it was 50/20. Not good at all.

I asked her, "Is he okay?"

She said, "Everything is going to be alright."

I asked her, "What is wrong?"

She began to share, he was having problems. His kidneys, bladder, liver, bowels and lungs were not working. They had shut down! He was not able to breathe on his own without life support. They had put him on a medication that would force his heart to beat. This medicine could only operate on the heart for no more than a twenty-four-hour window, due to the heart being a muscle. After that, it would no longer be effective. God had twenty-four hours to create a miracle.

In addition to this, she also shared Tommy had *sepsis*. Sepsis causes the organs in the body to shut down. Even with heavy antibiotics, only 20 percent of people survive. It is extremely dangerous!

I watched the nurse work vigorously on Tommy, moving back and forth in that small room. I felt I needed to go be alone for just a moment. I remembered the promise God had given me the day before, but I felt such a numb feeling. He said in three days he would rise up out of this. I knew he had come out, because God promised a whole miracle, not a part of a miracle. The truth of the matter was, the devil was not done yet and neither was God! I knew then that God was going to get the glory out of this!!!

I went back into the CCU waiting room. A woman from our ministry had been praying with us nightly. She was reading the Word that morning while she was waiting on me.

I sat down in the chair to think on the Lord. I felt the Spirit of the Lord urging me to go pray. I felt such an urgency that I even remember speaking it out loud to myself, "I need to go pray!"

The women who had been in prayer that day said, "We can go to the car or down the hall and pray."

The odd thing at that moment was, I felt the gift of faith and felt numb all at the same time. I told her, "Let's go down the hall and find a place to come into agreement in prayer."

I was joined with about twelve other men and women of God who were there and together we all went down the hall to pray. We knew it was serious and did not even think about being loud or bothering anyone. I needed a miracle and I knew our prayers would work.

We got to the end of the hall where there were double doors. We stopped right then and there. I faced the wall and I began to pray. I instantly felt the Lord. He was waiting on me. At that moment, I let the Holy Spirit pray through me.

Not knowing what to pray, but trusting in Him, He showed me a picture in my mind of a worm. It was not more than an inch long, and as I looked at it, the back side of the worm began to turn black. The blackness worked its way up the body of the worm and I knew in my heart (my knower) that the assignment from the enemy, his plan and activity, was dying.

I began to ask the Lord, "What are you showing me?" I did not completely understand at that time, but I knew God was showing me something.

I found out later from the medical field that under a microscope, sepsis looks like a worm. It looks just like what I saw. God showed me He had killed it. God blocked death and held it back! Like the song says, "God blocked it!"

All of a sudden, the Spirit of heavy prayer began to lift, and everyone began to get up from prayer. We no longer felt the need to pray. I knew at that moment the Lord had done the work that was needed. Thank you, Jesus!!!

We all joined back together, we began to share what we saw and heard from the Lord. The pastor that called me the day before that gave me the news, shared he saw Tommy at the gates of Heaven. He said he saw Tommy turning and saying, "Lord, please not yet. I have so much more to do." We did not realize until later on, around that same timeframe, Tommy was walking around Heaven.

Now that we had heard from the Lord, I went back to the CCU waiting room. I wanted to be with him and pray over him, but I *knew* everything was going to be alright now! I continued to take visitors back to see him and many of them would pray again, but I knew we had touched the Lord in prayer already. So, we praised and we waited for the manifestation of our prayers to come to fruition.

Yes, my mind would wander for a moment, but I never let it stay there. My spirit was heavy with assurance and there was no fear. I knew this was warfare and I had just won the battle over Tommy's life. Now we just had to wait on the manifestation of the healing.

Sunday, March 4, at 10:10 a.m., I will never forget it. I was in Tommy's room and the doctor came in with a report telling me it was a miracle Tommy was even alive. The second surgery was

> *Sometimes you have to wait. This was the road we were on at the time and we needed to strategically follow orders and the voice of God within.*

worse than the previous one. Tommy's organs had quit working for seventeen hours.

The doctor was amazed the sepsis was completely gone and that he was going to survive! He also said however, he would likely never function normally again; he would be a vegetable for the rest of his life. Well, we had heard this kind of report before, so earlier we had also heard from the creator of all things – everything was going to be alright!

Whose report will you believe? There is one thing you must learn, anything that is spoken against the Word of God must be ignored! You must realize there is no truth in it. When someone speaks against the Word of God, they are calling God a liar. You cannot be moved by what you think, feel, hear, or see. You *have to stand firmly believing* what the Word of God says!

What is more real than you and me? Who can heal, give peace, direction, faith, and a love that no one else can give? I know the answer to that question, and it is Jesus!

Now, I am not saying everyone should ignore the doctor's order, but if God has given you a promise, YOU HOLD ON TO IT! I am saying, while the physician has given you their medical prescription, take heed. I had to stay in the Word and in prayer. After God spoke to my heart with several confirmations, I waited for the Lord to prove Himself by the examination.

Sometimes you have to wait. This was the road we were on at the time and we needed to strategically follow orders and the voice of God within.

So, waiting once again, I knew I had a miracle ahead of me. They kept him asleep for the next three days as before. The process had begun all over again. Just as our pastor friend said would happen, "In three days the Lord will raise him up."

Chapter 13

The Arrival

Tommy

There were many times in life that I dreamt in the night of Jesus coming back in clouds just like I had read in the Bible, but this time I knew it was no dream. One time when I was very young I dreamt a trumpet blew and I even felt my body lift from my bed and head upwards toward the ceiling of my tiny bedroom, but I woke up before I left the house and I knew I was having a vivid dream of the rapture. This time was not like all the other times, this time was for real. All of my senses were active and normal. I was not asleep, I was definitely awake and aware that I had stepped into the beyond. My faculties were as they are right now while writing this book. Within moments, I just appeared instantly, walking down a country road on a whiter-than-snow, gravel-like substance. I had absolutely no apprehension and no fear of anything. As I ventured on my new excursion, I noticed there were no sharp edges in the gravel; nothing existed that would harm anyone or anything. The life we live today is filled with stickers and bruises, but this place had no thorns, no thistles, no splinters—nothing that could cause any physical pain. It simply did not exist!

> *On several occasions I have heard stories told over the years about people going to Heaven... Many people are fascinated by these types of stories, but for me...I knew I wanted to go to Heaven someday, but not today. I only wanted to go to Heaven in the rapture!*

On several occasions I have heard stories told over the years about people going to Heaven while on the operating table and their bodies floating in the room; looking down on themselves. Many of them expressed they went through a tunnel, and while going through this tunnel, a choir was singing, or there were bright lights everywhere. In their testimony, they always mentioned that they recognized they were in Heaven.

Many people are fascinated by these types of stories, but for me, they never captivated much of my attention. This was not my experience! I knew I wanted to go to Heaven someday, but not today, and furthermore, I only wanted to go to Heaven in the rapture!

But I have personally known people who have had similar experiences. In fact, my pastor when I was a child, Rev. J. C. Hibbard of the Gospel Lighthouse Church in Dallas, Texas experienced this. While on his deathbed with some of his family members standing around him, he passed away in their presence.

His wife explained to the congregation that their whole bedroom was filled with an amazing sound of rumbling wheels getting louder and louder as he was passing away. Someone standing by asked him what they were all hearing and right before he passed he explained they were hearing the wheels of the chariot that was coming to escort him into the heavenly realm. They said the rumbling wheels were so loud that everyone in the home could hear it, including those who were in different levels of the home.

Pastor Hibbard lived in a large renaissance styled home that set on the west side of Dallas. I am sure you can only imagine, in an approximately 7,000 square foot home how that must have echoed throughout the entire mansion. When he passed away, it was reported, the wheel sounds slowly faded away as they returned to where they had come from and he was gone.

I remember like it was yesterday when they told this to the church congregation in the following Sunday morning service. The moment they heard it, the whole congregation broke out in a shout, because our Pastor had crossed the finish line.

Again, this is not my story. My experience came with no delay, I was just there - in Heaven. As if I had been there many times before, I knew where I was, I knew I was in Heaven and I had crossed the finish line. It was like returning home after a long, long trip. Everything I saw and felt was familiar to me, with no explanations needed. Also, it was not a foreign place to me. It was exactly who I was right now on earth, but without flaws and without mystery. It was within a moment of time and I was walking in a terrestrial land of sudden peace and safety.

> *"For now we see through a*
> *glass, darkly; but then face to face:*
> *now I know in part; but then shall I know*
> *even as also I am known."*
>
> (1 Corinthians 13:12 KJV)

It will be somewhat difficult trying to compare the things in Heaven to the things here on earth, but I am going to do my best to explain to you what I saw.

"And God shall wipe away all tears from their eyes; and there shall be no more death, neither sorrow, nor crying, neither shall there be any more pain: for the former things are passed away."

(Revelation 21:4 KJV)

My experience begins with me standing on a pea gravel road just for a moment, then being drawn by this inner intuition to walk forward on this road I was standing on. I yielded to my inner feeling and made my move. While I was walking down that road, I noticed an amazing peace encompassed me, as though a warm blanket of comfort was wrapped around me. In all my life, I have never known such peace.

Peace was a normal way of life in my parents' home. There was no fighting, screaming, or even a raised voice at one another in my parents' house. In fact, they did not permit it at all. I was not raised in a rambunctious house filled with loud, unruly manners, so when I say the peace was beyond what I had ever experienced, I mean it was tranquil. The atmosphere was filled with this overpowering presence of love. Not an icky, sticky, gooey feeling, but a warm, calm atmosphere where absolutely nothing could ever hurt anyone ever again. It may be hard to grasp, but even the knowledge of fear, worry, depression, heartache, trouble, and torment did not exist. I did not even think at that moment that the negativity we are used to constantly being bombarded with every day, did not exist. It was not until I came back while lying in the hospital bed that it dawned on me that pain on any level does not exist. God does not permit it at all. There were no aches, sickness, or death — nothing negative had the permission to exist.

The phrase, "the peace that passes all understanding" mentioned in the Bible, opened up before my very eyes. The peace of mind I experienced was overwhelming like a warm blanket wrapped around me. There was this never-ending, overwhelming restfulness intermingled with inner joy. Feeling this never-ending sense of strong, loving arms wrapped around me and I knew all at the same time, it was Him.

> *"and the peace of God, which surpasses all understanding, will guard your hearts and minds through Christ Jesus."*
>
> (Philippians 4:7 NKJV)

So many have asked me questions, and the most common one is, what is the weather like? Well, heat and I do not get along. Matter of fact, I do not even like summertime because I do not like hot weather at all. Every time someone says they like the hot days of summer I think, *oh my, not me!*

I prefer the cooler days of the fall season, so for me, the weather was perfect. There was a light breeze that seemed to carry a worshipful atmosphere. The clouds were white, fluffy, cotton-like and the sky was bluer than I had ever seen before. Continuing the walk, a soft, breeze seemed to follow me everywhere I went which made everything happy and content. It was a place a person would never want to leave. I am one of those types of people who look forward to the seasons that seem to blow in the fresh air. You know, the kind of day that makes you want to place a blanket on the ground and stretch, or the kind of day that would have been perfect for flying a kite- that was this day!

For a moment I noticed there was no dust anywhere around. Coming from a dusty Texas town where much of the time you do a lot of sneezing, I was amazed there was no dust in the air. Everything there was clean and spotless. You might even say even the air was sanctified. I was reminded of the passage of scripture Ephesians 5:27, Jesus will present her (His bride, the church) to Himself as a glorious church without spot or wrinkle or any other blemish. Instead, she will be holy and without fault.

> "That He might present her to Himself a glorious church, not having spot or wrinkle or any such thing, but that she should be holy and without blemish."
> (Ephesians 5:27 NKJV)

I am sure everyone has had to pay that miserable light bill every month. You know as well as I do, if you do not pay the bill, you will not have any electricity. The electric company has aggravated me many times. You pay your bill and they fight with you anyway, but the great news is, there are no bill payments in Heaven. They are all paid in full.

Speaking of electricity, Heaven was encompassed by a glowing light, an endless power that required no electricity. This power source came only from Jesus Himself and I was made aware of it.

Mentioning lighting, shadows did not exist. Shadows require an item or someone standing in one place and the light remaining in another place, shining only on one side of that image. Imagine yourself standing in a doorway with the sun behind you and the light casting its way around you. The illumination of the light will then cast a shadow into the house, but not in Heaven.

The glory of God is everywhere all at the same time. Since He is omnipresent, He is at one place and yet His glory is all around, no matter where you are standing or walking, He is there.

Since God Himself and His glory are one and the same, the light is equally the same everywhere you turn. The presence of the Lord is everywhere. His light is everywhere. Since His light is everywhere, there are no shadows. The light of the Lord is equally brilliant everywhere, all in the same place; He is omnipresent.

> Every living thing, every living soul looks up to Him as their sole provider. Even the little flowers looked to Him with great adoration. Their entire desire was to worship Jesus; the only thing everything wanted to do with all their heart was to worship Him.

And he showed me a pure[a] river of water of life, clear as crystal, proceeding from the throne of God and of the Lamb. In the middle of its street, and on either side of the river, is the tree of life, which bore twelve fruits, each tree yielding its fruit every month. The leaves of the tree were for the healing of the nations.

(Revelation 22:1-2 NKJV)

Notice the words, every month and every season brings a beautiful change. There is never a dull moment or boring day. In His presence there is fullness of joy.

This particular summer-autumn was not hot at all; it was perfect. It actually made me think of the ending of summer-autumn in the Hawaiian Islands because I enjoy snow skiing, I especially loved the mountains. The peaks were over-laden with the whitest, untainted snow and at the lower level, fields were glistening emerald green fields that sparkled in the light. The seasons were perfect. Actually, everything was perfect.

Several years ago, Karen, Joshuia and I held a church service in Kentucky. I had never been to that part of our country before, so seeing blue grass for the first time was pretty amazing. Before then, I had only seen photos of the beautiful grassland. It has this unforgettable, unique color of soft emerald green blades that is not only attractive to the eyes, but to the touch as well. These fields of grass were much like the Kentucky blue grass with tiny fireflies hanging on the tips of some of the blades. Even though I did not get down on my knees and get an up-close look at the grass, I knew each blade had its own personality; its own distinct handy work of art that God made with all His divine wisdom and perfection.

There were flowers everywhere! Each of them had a childlike personality. It was as though they had a playful, happy life themselves. The faces of the flowers looked as though they could have looked up at me and spoken. They did not talk, but it would not have surprised me at all if they had stood up on their petals and sang a song. They, like everything else, carried the same sweetness of the Spirit of God Himself.

Every living thing, every living soul looks up to Him as their sole provider. Even the little flowers looked to Him with great adoration. Their entire desire was to worship Jesus; the only thing everything wanted to do with all their heart was to worship Him. There was not anything or anyone that did not give Him attention and adoration.

Have you ever been somewhere and had the feeling, *Hmmm? I feel like I have been here before?* Well, I have had that experience many times in my life. I realize at that very moment, I was submerged in God's presence. Each time I had prayed a prayer or worshipped the Lord, it placed me in front of His throne. I know clearer now than ever before that those special times of visitation I have experienced had placed me in the exact same spot I was standing in when I went to Heaven. Finally, I saw with my own eyes the place I had been many times before in prayer. It was amazing! This is why I said I had been there before.

Through my years of intercession through the power of prayer and worship, I have been overtaken by His glory. Being in Heaven surrounded by His existence, was much the same, only deeper and visual. I was now walking in the realm I had only been in while in the spirit of prayer.

Can you remember one time in your life where the Spirit of God moved on your heart and you thought, "If I could just actually live in this peaceful place, I would never leave?" Well, that is where I was. During my prayer time, my petitions leave my heart in faith, representing my need, before the presence of God. This time was not through prayer, but instead, I finally reached the portal that elevated me into the tangible presence of God. There is absolutely no power in hell that can overtake anyone in His presence. I finally had made it to Heaven!

Continuing to walk on, I saw three men heading toward me. I immediately recognized who they were, as if we were old friends. There was no need for introductions, because I instantly knew they had been watching over me my whole life. I knew they had been my guardian angels.

Chapter 14

Three Angels

Tommy

To describe what I am about to tell you is very hard. I am explaining a place that is very real but very supernatural. A place that has been created by Jesus. The human mind cannot conceive the supernatural without the Spirit revealing these things to them.

I looked up and heading my direction were three angelic men, and they were dressed in pearly white attire that glistened from head to toe as they walked. Their robes shimmered in the light that gave off a sparkling, glimmering light. On their heads they wore turbans with a single jewel hanging down in the center of their foreheads and long, ornate tunics that draped down with sort of puff over-pants that reached down to their feet. Their shoes were covered with sterling silver fabric intertwined with pure golden filigree thread and inlaid with brilliant stones. The front of the shoes curled upward, with a single precious stone, about a three-inch diameter teardrop diamond, hanging from the tip of the curl. The stones were flawless. Not only were they perfect in beauty, every stone was of the highest quality grade. Semi-precious stones that do not exist just anywhere; only the best for God and His royal entourage.

Their garments were made with interwoven flexible diamonds and other precious gems. The diamonds crinkled with the fabric as the garments moved. These particular heavenly diamonds were not hard as they are on earth; and when the fabric was released, it left no wrinkles, no creases. I also noticed there were no seams. Then I remembered the Bible described Jesus' robe as seamless; the best money could buy in that day. When I saw there were no wrinkles in the fabric of their clothes,

I instinctively knew that wrinkles do not exist there, because they represent a defiled church. Wrinkles represent imperfection, uncared for garments, and there are no imperfections in God's presence.

The angelic men who walked with me were powerful with great rank and authority. These men walked with stately stride and grace. These guys were on a mission; they took their position and rank very seriously. They greeted me upon my arrival with a kind nod of the head and a genuine smile, and we headed back the way from which they had come. I could never have come up with in my imagination the elaborate things I saw, even though I have been told my entire life that I have a very colorful imagination sometimes.

> *As the four of us walked together, I instantly knew if there was something I wanted done, I was to give the order, and these three angels would see to it.*

The mission of these angels was to escort me wherever I wanted to go. Do not take this the wrong way, these men were not in my life to be my butlers and guides. A better way to describe them is they were my assistants. They had the greatest spirit and attitude about them, they did not carry an arrogant air. These were the "good guys," and I am glad they walked with me! They were a part of my inheritance as an overcomer. An overcomer is one who accepts Jesus as his or her Savior, believing He died and rose again for him or her. An overcomer equips themselves with training to win the race of life that we all are born to run. He who is an overcomer ends his or her life achieving the will of God and gaining the eternal crown when the race is completed.

You see, they belong to Jesus, and He had given them strict orders to taken care of me, watch over me and my life.

Although they were gentle and kind, they were also serious about their position. It was quite obvious they were not playing around even though at times they were light hearted and funny. One of the three was more of a character, like someone who enjoyed jokes. He laughed a lot, but never rude or out of order.

He was definitely fun to be with and I cannot wait to see him again. He and I will probably spend several millennium's kicking up our heels and rolling on the floor; the golden floor that is. The angel in the middle had very high seniority. He spoke more often to me the other two. The angels walking on the outside of the one in the middle, held seniority over all the other angels I saw. They did not speak to me much; they mostly spoke to the one in charge, and he spoke to me. They were not scary as some may think, but I knew they could cause a problem quickly should someone try to overtake the Kingdom of God. They were all very holy, even the funny one. Of course, we all know committing treason will never happen. God is in charge forever.

There are several scriptures in the Bible that describes where God's angels are equipped with authority and power to overtake the enemies of God. One angel alone caused thousands to lose their eyesight in a battle which allowed Israel to win that war. I definitely want to be their friend, not their opponent. I fear them in the Lord, but I also respect them. Many times in my life they kept me from harm. I cannot express enough gratitude for the multiple times God spared my life from tragic events that could have been a lot worse than they turned out. Thank you, Jesus, for your angelic protection.

For the first time in my life I really understood kingdom protocol, as I saw it in action for myself. Everything worked together and in order, orchestrated by the principles of the kingdom of God. No one was rude, and no one was unruly. Everything and everyone had its place and office without murmur and complaint. It all worked smoothly as clock work and was designed to be on God's timeframe.

Heaven is run by Him, and everything is ruled by chain of command with strict protocol without the headache. Just like any other earthly monarchy, Heaven has a King and Lords. We are the children of the Most High, and we are the only ones free to live as children. So, we answer to Jesus only. Many times I imagine what it would be like to be an heir to the throne of England, especially since I found out my mother's ancestry line is from King Richard the Lionheart. Funny as it may seem, when I was a child, I would throw a towel or blanket around me and pretend I was a king of a very wealthy empire. In God's Empire, He is the only true and living God and is very loving and not a tyrant like Pharaoh was in Egypt. That ruler, according to the Bible was a hard taskmaster. God is not like that at all. He is kind and loving, pure and devoted. I am so glad He calls me His son.

It was at that time that my angelic friends led me further down the road. Carrying on with our conversation, after a few steps were taken, I looked up. About two blocks ahead of us stood a fortified wall that was at least ten feet thick and so high one could not climb to the top of it. Maybe if I had stood far away, I would have been able to see the top of this wall, but I was not sure. My heart raced with excitement with every step we took, seeing new things I had never seen before.

When I looked up from the road, I saw a wall surrounding an estate; I knew it was my estate! The wall was made from pure white stone, something like marble or alabaster with colorful veins running through it. It was the most majestic and beautiful stone I had ever seen. It wrapped around the estate as a wall of protection even though there was not any need for protection.

I took time to walk around the wall before I entered. I walked through the gates and they were massive in stature and remained open all the time.

> *Its gates shall not be shut at all*
> *by day (there shall never be any night there).*
>
> *(Revelation 21:25 NKJV)*

There was never any need to close these gates, because there were no enemies and no nighttime there. We all are aware of that eerie feeling insecurity brings that causes people to lock doors on earth, but this threat does not exist in this place. You know it may be hard for some to believe, but I remember when I was a child, my parents never locked the doors of our house in Dallas back in the 60s and the 70s. There was no need or thought of it until I was older. A lot has changed since then, but Heaven never ever changes and does not endorse break-ins. The streets are safe and secure.

Perpetrators, thieves and anything or anyone who would bring harm are not allowed in the kingdom of Christ. You will not find hospitals, burglar bars, and no security systems anywhere in that city where the Son of God is the light! These things were not needed because thieves and the like were not allowed to live in this Heavenly world! God is a good Father and He has created a place that is eternally safe and happy for those who remain faithful to Him until the end. I have come back to tell you that Heaven will be worth whatever you have to endure to get there.

The moment I arrived I had an instant knowledge that this estate was part of my inheritance. It was all mine, yet there was no ownership involved. As much as it was mine, it was God's: it was ours together just as in a marriage.

It is a covenant relationship between God and ourselves, like a marriage. Everything my parents left me on earth became equally my wife's, because we were married. We are one. In that same way, what belongs to me, belongs to Jesus. It does not really matter to me anyway as long as I get to be with Him, right?

I belong to Him and He belongs to me. He made an everlasting covenant with those who made the choice to be one with Him. I am the righteousness of God in Christ Jesus (2 Corinthians 5:21). He has made me an heir and a joint heir with Him. We really need to understand this one truth: our inheritance is not Heaven; our inheritance is Jesus. What a great inheritance. I mean, if we have Jesus, we have it all!

For He made Him who knew no sin to be sin for us, that we might become the righteousness of God in Him.

(2 Corinthians 5:21)

When you have Him, you have access to everything that belongs to Him because you are one with God in Christ.

Chapter 15

☀ The Estate

Tommy

As we left the gravel road that surrounded the walls of marble, we entered through the gate. A vast, majestic courtyard opened in front of me. In my line of sight there were three buildings surrounding the outer parameters of the courtyard. There was a very large, alabaster, round, ornate three-tier fountain that was about eight feet in diameter and twelve feet in height placed so perfectly in the center of the courtyard. Then I noticed the courtyard floor.

The floor was made of the same material as the wall. It looked as though it had been broken in small and large pieces before it was laid then placed back together again with no indentions, no cracks, and no rough edges.

It drew my attention so that I bent down to touch it. It was smooth and beautiful. There were no flaws you could feel with the hand. Under the surface; however, were broken pieces inlaid in the flooring. These pieces represented the times on earth where I had been broken and hurt in my life. The smooth surface represented a covering over those pieces because the Lord had healed me and put me back together.

Marks and scars were there, but He had removed the pain. Standing there I knew what every line represented and could remember when I went through those events, but there were no side effects, no pain, and no more hurt.

Looking to the left of me, there stood a large building made of alabaster with marble columns all the way around.

I walked up a few steps and entered the foyer of the building. One of the first things I noticed was the decorated walls that were completely lined with beautiful, different sizes of oil paintings. Looking at the paintings, I saw exquisite colors surrounded by gold frames. There was one painting that stuck out to me that was like a landscape of trees and rolling hills.

Instantly, I knew I could step into the painting and walk around and be immediately in a different dimension of Heaven, if I chose to. The painting was alive: a type of portal from one place to the next, none of which would never take me out of the presence of God. He was in every dimension.

> *The city is laid out as a square;*
> *its length is as great as its breadth.*
> *And he measured the city with the reed:*
> *==twelve thousand furlongs. Its length,==*
> *==breadth, and height are equal.==*
>
> *(Revelations 21:16 NKJV)*

Entering the main room, it was absolutely beautiful. It was rectangular in shape and vast in depth and height. There were very large marble columns which were so large my arms would not reach around them. They reached from the ceiling to the floor and lined the walkway from the front of the room to the back of the room.

When I looked up, there was a second level that surrounded the same perimeter, with the same pillars stretching to the top. There were carved crowns on the top of each column that were made of marble or alabaster. The entire ceiling was exquisite with an oil-painted mural of angels, flowers and clouds.

This particular room was where social gatherings would take place and the Lord knows I love parties. There were three separate seating areas with beautiful furniture, that of which only kings would own. Underneath the furniture laid rugs with brilliant colors we are familiar with, as well as colors only known to God. They were beautiful and placed gracefully in perfect position on the floor. The colors were breathtaking. They were made with wool and interwoven silk of hot pink and royal blue.

Everything I experienced fit my taste and personality right down to the intricate details. This place reminded me of a hotel I had stayed at in Hawaii called the Royal Hawaiian. The grandeur and magnificent handiwork at the Royal Hawaiian was museum quality all the way down to the coral colored walls. That hotel was lavished with exotic island flowers and colors only God could come up with and the buildings I am writing about were much more exquisite.

Later on, when I awakened in the hospital; I was shown a penny. Looking at the backside of the coin, I said to my wife, "I just came from there." In the state I was in at that time, I did not realize it was the Lincoln Memorial. All I knew was the image on that coin was much the same as one of the buildings from where I had just come.

Chapter 16

The Promised Land

Tommy

I walked out the massive doorway of that columned building and stepped back into the front courtyard. The buildings were arranged inside the walls facing the courtyard. The large Lincoln Memorial-type building, which I had just been standing in, was on the left as I walked through the gate.

To the right of that building was a smaller building facing the gate. This building was made in the same architectural design as the first building. I did not go into this one, but knew it was my prayer chamber where private worship and prayer could be made. I knew this place intertwined with the prayer room I had on earth. When I went into my place of prayer in my earthly home, in the spirit, this is where my prayers were taking place in Heaven.

The third building was to the right of the prayer chamber, facing the first large building. It was not as small as the prayer building and not as large as the first building on the left, but it was the same style as the others. This last building was living quarters or a mansion. I do not know why I never went into this building, but I know it is waiting on me to come back home someday soon.

Standing at the courtyard gate and looking out from the entrance; in front of me were several large vineyards on magnificent rolling hills as far as the eyes could see. Part of these vineyards belonged to my estate and the vineyards were overseen by angelic servants.

They, like the ones who greeted me, were tall in stature and strong. They had no wings, like many on earth have painted them. They looked just like men. They wore ivory colored work robes with burgundy sashes wrapped around their waists. While working they would take the length of their robes and tuck them inside the sashes, which made them look like britches.

All of them were hard at work and there was not a lazy one among them. Funny thing was, I noticed they were not perspiring from their labor. It was because the curse of working by the sweat of the brow does not exist there.

In the sweat of thy face shalt thou
eat bread, till thou return unto the ground; for
out of it wast thou taken: for dust thou art,
and unto dust shalt thou return.
(Genesis 3:19 NKJV)

The grapevines were overloaded and heavy with fruit. Every single grape was about the size of a plum, similar to when Joshua's and Caleb's men came back from the Promised Land carrying a large cluster of grapes on one pole on each of their shoulders.

When they reached the Valley of Eshcol, they cut off a branch bearing a single cluster of grapes. Two of them carried it on a pole between them, along with some pomegranates and figs. They were so heavy the men had to walk at a slow pace as to not break the pole and lose all the grapes.

Then they came to the Valley of Eshcol, and there cut down a branch with one cluster of grapes; they carried it between two of them on a pole. They also brought some of the pomegranates and figs. (Numbers 13:23 NKJV)

The wind blew around me with the same playful attitude as a puppy...The sound it made was voices of worship, giving Him continual praise for everything He has done and His ability to produce an unending supply of creativity to show how marvelous He is.

Much like the Biblical story, my vineyard was filled with gatherers. They were all very busy working and overseeing the vineyard, paying close attention to their work. They were serious, and it definitely was not playtime, but rather, a time of preparing for the greatest event ever known in history on earth or in Heaven.

Many gatherers were getting ready for harvest time. I knew deep inside my heart there was going to be a party soon, and the grapes were being gathered in order to be crushed into the finest wine ever known to man. A celebration was just around the corner, and everyone was working hard to get it all done in time. They were preparing for the wedding of the King. By everything I saw, it was going to be extremely elaborate to celebrate the King and all His children.

These gatherers were men with great power, and they were given to serve, not as slaves, but as overseers that went with the estate. The slavery mentality did not exist anywhere; there were only those with a servant's heart. While there, I understood a lot of things the Bible speaks of more clearly, such as when Jesus said, "The greatest in His Father's Kingdom are those with a servant's heart" (Matthew 23:11), the greatest among you will be servants.

> *But he who is greatest*
> *among you shall be your servant.*
> *(Matthew 23:11 NKJV)*

I guess I had stood there long enough, because my heart knew it was time to move on. The three angelic men I met when I arrived stayed to finish what they were working on, and I left through the gate, traveling farther down the soft-gravel road by myself from that moment on.

Even though I am by myself at this point, after being led by someone in the beginning of my walk, I was not with the feeling of abandonment. I knew I still was not walking alone. I still had Jesus at my side, even though I had not seen Him yet. I felt Him all around me. I feel Him right now while typing this book here in my home. He is an ever-present help in the time of trouble. We are never alone!

Coming from the heavenly atmosphere to the right of me, I heard two separate distinct sweet sounds at the same time, which united to make one sound of wind, like two small voices blowing in harmony.

The wind blew around me with the same playful attitude as a puppy would have when it wanted to play. It circled around my head and shoulders. I felt the wind blow through my ears. The sound it made was voices of worship, giving Him continual praise for everything He has done and His ability to produce an unending supply of creativity to show how marvelous He is. He is unending! He is infinite! The wind whispered His wonderful name and His marvelous works.

For example, envision blowing softly with your mouth and at the same time singing a beautiful song. That is what it was like. At that moment, I was encompassed with an extreme feeling of joy and peace. If I had stayed just to play with the wind, that alone would have been enough of a heavenly experience about which to have written.

I have wished several times that I could have recorded the sounds and the views of all I saw and heard. The trees were picturesque and varied, like we have here on earth. The difference here though, was among the trees that had leaves of green, were also trees with leaves made of precious stones, living stones with all kinds of colors and all types of trees.

The trees with stoned leaves were alive with veins running through them, like we see in green trees, but their leaves were completely made of precious stone! The one that drew my attention was an amber tree with exquisite deep colors of reds and orange. The colors of the leaves seemed to scream with His brilliant imagination that comes to life when He speaks His Word. The leaf that was made of stone was not translucent, and when the light hit the leaf, it glistened. By this tree, I knew it was autumn, or about to be.

All the colors in Heaven were sharper and more intense than any brilliant color on earth; and each portrayed His personality. Those colors were not only radiant, but they were alive.

Everything had His touch and its own testimony of His glory and His love. It is very hard to describe with words and explain but think of it as an artist painting a picture on canvas. Everything the artist paints, every stroke, comes from his imagination.

You never know what the artist is thinking until you hand

him a paintbrush and some paint. The artist then goes to work describing what he sees in his mind.

Can you imagine if everything you painted instantly came to life and was not simply a painting of rolling hills and trees? Imagine the very life of God entered the painting as it was being transferred to the canvas. This is what happens in Heaven!

Chapter 17

I See Him

Tommy

From the flowers, to the majestic colors, even down to the structures of the walls, God created Heaven to exhibit how much love He has for man. Every intricate detail was like careful brush strokes in an artist's painting; revealing His true thoughts concerning me.

I am not so sure about everyone else, but when it comes to me, when I truly love someone, I give my all! I do not just say I care about that person or say, "I love you," but it is important to me to prove it to that individual. It is important to me to show it to the very best of my ability.

The more I love someone, the more of me they have access to. This is just how Jesus is. I could see His love with my eyes and touch it with my hands. I experienced the depth and the height of God's love for me, and the whole human race, first hand.

This is how God feels about you: He has only *God-sized love!*

Love suffers long and is kind;

love does not envy; love does not parade

itself, is not puffed up;

(1 Corinthians 13:4 NKJV)

Since this describes love from the human point of view, you can only imagine what Jesus feels. He not only loves, but He is also the very definition of love.

He is crazy about man! His expression of that love is exhibited everywhere. It is in everything; even in the breeze.

Everything I experienced had many meanings and interpretations when I was there, and I had no trouble understanding them all. It will just be something you will know the very moment you arrive.

I continued walking down the road and about twenty feet in front of me was an open field of grass with a few large stones. There were people who gathered there, but not in one single group. The crowds of people were having conversations in a relaxed environment, which was overseen by the Great Shepherd. I am sure you have been to a few picnic gatherings in your life where some of the adults were sitting around talking while the younger groups were playing games and the kids were chasing each other around. Jesus was always around, enjoying their laughter and activity. I could tell He enjoyed that they were having an incredible time with one another. He is not a hard taskmaster, but a friend, the Good Shepherd.

Over to the right of me were a couple of men playing a game, much like Frisbee here, while there were some people sitting on the ground talking; some were having a picnic. It was like a park area where you would go and enjoy friends and family.

They were dressed casually. Most of the garments were white, but some of the garments had color. Some wore pants while others wore robes; there were even some with knee-length pants on. Their clothes never got dirty and smudges never appeared, those do not exist there. They never got wrinkled or sweaty. The fabric was perfect all the time. It was a perfect day.

> *In Heaven, there is no such thing as offense. It does not exist.*

I turned and looked over my right shoulder and saw Jesus sitting on a large boulder with one leg propped up underneath Him; His foot resting against the stone on which He was seated. A man stood talking with Jesus and, even though I could not hear their conversation, I observed Jesus's eyes were attentive to that man, because it was important to him.

Jesus was aware I had just walked up and was standing in the distance. I felt His eyes on me as a loving friend or a watchman, but not just on me, but also over everything and everyone all at the same time. While standing by and watching for a moment, I was encompassed by great peace beyond anything I had ever known.

There were times I heard the sounds of laughter from what sounded to me like children playing in the distance. At the same time there was a quiet breeze and peaceful serenity that is so hard to explain. Only the Lord can make both possible all at the same time. It was just a wonderful day, that day at the park. It was one of those special days that no one wants to end.

Interestingly, it was not until a couple of days later laying in the hospital bed that I realized Jesus had spoken to that man privately, right in front of me, and I was not offended at all. I was taught all my life that it is completely rude to whisper in front of others or to speak in the company of others in a low tone, because it could cause them to think you were talking negatively about them.

In Heaven, there is no such thing as offense. It does not exist. This became very important to me, because I had never before thought about it. I was in the presence of the King, and I did not even realize that it did not matter if He had spoken secrets to me in front of others. No one ever gets offended in Heaven.

Trust me, you will never be disappointed or hurt again. Heaven is so wonderful, and Jesus is even greater!

Then it was time for me to walk on. The crowd was now behind me, where the Lord was sitting on the large stone. Still, I felt as though He was *right next* to me, even though I had walked on. The best way to describe it is that the life we live on earth demands oxygen. We cannot breathe without it. Though we cannot see it, it does exist.

His omnipresence is like our oxygen. Not only will we collapse, we eventually die without it. Heaven's oxygen is God's presence. There is no way to live without it. This is the same presence that comes in a smaller measure in a sweet church service when we worship Him. I cannot see oxygen, nor can I see the presence of God. Just because I cannot see air does not mean it does not exist. Just because we cannot see His presence does not mean it does not exist.

He is the atmosphere in Heaven. He is everything for which all the kingdom reigns. His glory, or presence, is what everyone and everything breathes.

As I continued to walked, I happened to see the most amazing field of wheat. I am not sure if that was something the Spirit of God was showing as a vision or if it was an actuality. After this experience, I do believe it was a vision concerning the future of the coming hour for us here on earth. I came to a standstill and was in awe. There was a field of golden wheat, and the stalks had faces. They were crying and bending backwards from the force of the wind that was beginning to blow.

Looking ahead of me in the near distance, I saw huge, dark, angry clouds coming my direction. The wheat was filled with fear for their lives. Something deep inside me knew it was about to become violent, and I knew harvest time was about to pass. It was very soon going to be too late.

The interpretation was instantly given to me and I knew the wheat represented the souls of people and how so many have been overlooked. Harvest time was soon to be over.

When I saw just how close we were to the end of time, I knew by that alone that we, the Church, had better get into the harvest field and reap as much as we possibly could because Jesus would be coming very, very soon!

Chapter 18

His Eyes

Tommy

After the vision was completed, Jesus came to me. I was escorted without anyone's assistance, and instantly before Him.

He was kind and considerate, and He radiated love. *He is Love.* You cannot separate the two; they are one and the same. When I saw Him, I realized a lot of things I had not seen before. He was the answer to *all* of life's questions and problems, and without Him nothing was made.

All things were made through Him, and without Him nothing was made that was made.

(John 1:3 NKJV)

He is life. There is no life outside of Him; it does not exist anywhere.

He wore the whitest, most pearl robe, which extended all the way down to His ankles. His shoes were tan colored leather-like sandals. There was an iridescent sash wrapped around Him that was purplish-blue which changed colors as He moved. The colors had life deep inside them as though they were alive themselves, and they represented the whole human race He had created.

His robe flowed softly as He walked. It is as if the robe was itself alive. We are His body, and His robe is His Father's authority, and He alone is all in all things.

His hair was brown and thick, with highlights that were all-natural colors. It was just above shoulder length and it had strong, thick waves. He was about six feet tall and had broad shoulders.

Several people have asked me the question, "What color is His skin?" Actually, why it would matter to anyone, has always been my question. He is so beautiful in character and full of honor and glory, why would anyone care what color of skin Jesus has? He created every color known and unknown to man. It all comes from within Him, but to answer the question, He was of an olive complexion. Maybe when I go back I can get Him to let me have His color of skin as well. I have always wanted to have a tan that never faded away.

He was very calm, confident, and loving. He was very gentle, with a strong personality, all at the same time. His compassion was overwhelming; almost intoxicating.

He was in charge, but not arrogant. He had no proud air of any kind and He was distracted by no one. I had His complete attention, while He had everything else to watch over. He was not overwhelming, just confident and kind.

Out of *all* that was shown on the journey to Heaven, and as beautiful as it was, I will never forget how overwhelmed I became when I saw His eyes.

His eyes!

They were captivating to the point I felt myself being drawn to Him and Him alone. I have never seen such beautiful eyes! I have never felt such a piercing gaze from someone as I did from Him. He knew me - every part of me from inside out. There was no condemnation; there was no fear. I was drawn to Him; I was drawn into His eyes.

Looking deep into His eyes I saw the throne of God and God Himself. I saw the deep pool of the source of all that love is— liquid love looking at me. I knew how crazy in love Jesus was with the human race. I instantly knew no matter what we had done, it would never change how much God was consumed with mankind.

Trust me, He is not a figment of the imagination. He is very real. He is breathtaking! He is power, He is love, He is war, and He is tender all at the same time.

We are not created to be His toys, but His closest companions, His friends. This does not mean, because He loves us, we can sin and live rebelliously without remorse. He loved us with *all* of His life. It made me begin to wonder. Do I love Him with *all* of mine? He died for me; am I willing to die for Him? He gave me *His all*. I have to freely give Him *my all!* It is not how much He loves me, but how much I love Him.

Here I was surrounded by *Him* alone, and there was no way any harm would come. The safest place in the entire known universe is in Christ. Suddenly, a safe *nowhere place* encompassed me. I was not floating, or on clouds; I was just *there*, suspended somewhere before Him. It was comfortable, like my hand in His. There was no sound from His voice, but I heard every word He spoke to me.

I heard Him say, "You can either come in and stay with me or go back and finish the work I gave you to do."

Now, please note that I never thought of my son or my wife while in Heaven and with Jesus—not because I do not love them, but because in Him, there is fullness of life.

The moment I knew there was still more that I could do for Him, I told Him, "I will go back and finish the work."

The next thing I knew, I was waking up in the hospital. I was supposed to have died on that table, but God had a different plan. I had to come back to tell you about Jesus and this wonderful place called Heaven. I would not miss it for the world if I were you!

Chapter 19

The Wait

Karen

During our three-day waiting period, I pulled out the worship music as before. This became my private prayer time with the Lord. It was a very quiet three days and it went really fast this time. It was as if I skipped over two days; it was amazing! I figured, if it worked once, it will work again. I knew what God had done just 10 days ago, in his first brain surgery. I believed God would finish up what He started. He does not leave His work undone.

One of Tommy's best friends, Pastor Milton Spears, came and shaved Tommy's face as he slept. He spoke into Tommy's life and told him about the miracle God was performing while praying over him. We knew Tommy's spirit could hear everything that was being said.

> The third day the doctors removed the breathing tube. When they woke Tommy this time, he spoke right away. One of the first things that he spoke was, "I have been somewhere, and I have a lot to tell you."

I was told by some of the nurses that it was possible Tommy (his flesh, this time) could hear me. So, I was always careful what was said around him. I made sure it was faith and always about the goodness of the Lord. This was not the time for negativity or confusion. His room had enough battles around it; he did not need anymore. I wanted his mind and his spirit bathed in a positive, heavenly atmosphere at all times.

I believed as the doctors and nurses did their thing and we did what we could, God would do His work and we would come out of this battle on top. There may be several battle scars, but we win the war!

Tuesday, March 6, "the third day," the doctors removed the breathing tube. When they woke Tommy this time, he spoke right away. One of the first things that he spoke was, "I have been somewhere, and I have a lot to tell you." The doctors were amazed that not only could he speak, but that he spoke well!

Tommy's head began to swell. When things rise against you after the promise has been given, you have to learn not to let these things affect your faith. The swelling became as large as a grapefruit. It was from the tissue in his brain, so they placed a small tube inside where the swelling was. Finally, it began to drain on its own. God was still performing miracles, one right after another, and we were getting to see the miracle play out before our very eyes!

Wednesday, March 7, Tommy was moved to the lower unit in ICU. Interestingly enough, the number "7" is God's number of completion. I knew then we would never be back for another

==brain surgery.== This may be a little far-fetched for some, but I was holding on to everything I could. I knew this was no coincidental move. It was complete this time. The recovery process started all over again and he had to ==relearn to sit, stand and walk==; all the basic, physical routines of daily life.

He responded so differently than the last time. I could feel the difference. Every day, three times a day, they would come in and help him sit, stand, walk, and work on the cognitive development of the brain.

He would have to recite the alphabet backward and recall things to help him with his thinking. They would have him say the months of the year backward as well. His memory was not the best, but he answered everything they asked correctly and in order. He did this every day. He was growing stronger and stronger.

His cognitive function was sharper than before, and we no longer had to call him pastor to get a response, but now he would answer to his name. He knew where he was and why he was there. Day after day they worked with Tommy to improve walking and normal everyday function. He was using a walker once again to relearn how to balance himself.

The difference between this surgery and the last was like night and day. He was regaining skills and recovering faster than before. He even started feeding himself for the first time since he was on the feeding tube. I knew death was behind him and life was in front of him. The Lord had given us victory over death.

The nurse came in on Sunday, March 11, and shared that a blood clot had developed in his leg. He would have to have a small procedure done to put a device in his vein called a filter (a small item that looks like a tiny gate) to keep the blood clot from traveling into the main artery in the chest area.

We continued to focus on our miracle.

You have to stay focused if you want to receive your miracle. You cannot lose sight of the promise God gives you; instead you must walk in the Spirit. It is like standing in front of Him and unzipping his body and stepping into Him, then zipping Him up with you inside.

I always make sure I created an atmosphere that was conducive for the Lord to be in our presence. Sometimes it was with heavy prayer, other times it was a lot of reading the Word.

There are times when you must stand on what you know. The time you have spent learning the voice of God, and through the investment you have made in the Word of God, ensure that moments in Him will never be in vain.

In the second surgery, prayer was so different. We had to war heavily in the Spirit of prayer. We prayed day and night, continually allowing God to speak to us. It was not that we did not pray continually during first surgery, but the attack of the enemy was so different.

I repeated everything upon which the Lord had given me to stand. I had to allow those things to be a large part of the very fiber of my being. I drew my strength from God and certainly know we would not be here today if the Lord had not spoken into our lives.

Tommy went through intense therapy every single day. While they kept him exercising to help develop his cognitive ability, I would read and pray. Once again, the nurses would come in and make comments about the atmosphere of our room and talk about the difference in his room from the rest of the hospital.

Certain people would come into his room and bring with them their own personal struggles. These issues would fight with Tommy and me every time they would come in the door. I was not about to allow stuff like hate, bitterness and unforgiveness to step into our room. I would not allow anyone to argue or bring in an attitude of confusion.

If any friends or family were not in agreement with me, I would not let them stay long. I would have to pray that peace would return, and the anointing of God would stay. I would plead the blood of Jesus over the room throughout the day so that God would hover over Tommy and stay in the room, especially at night.

> *"They shall take some of the blood and put it on the doorpost and the lintel of the houses in which they eat it."*
>
> (Exodus 12:7 NKJV)

> *"When the Lord goes through the land to strike down the Egyptians, He will see the blood on the top and the side of the door frame and he will pass over that doorway, and He will not permit the destroyer to enter your house and to strike you down."*
>
> *(Exodus 12:23 NIV)*

I knew that having the presence of God in the room would create a great miracle. To do this, we had to create an atmosphere where He felt invited. I made sure my relationship with Jesus was right. Along with prayer, Bible reading, and worship music, I made room for God. I certainly wanted Him to feel like He belonged wherever we were. So, His presence remained and caused there to be peace, assurance, and rest.

We trusted Him implicitly that the miracle would be completed in Tommy.

Chapter 20

God Covers Us

Karen

Friday, March 9, the doctor came in and said it was time to move to an in-house rehabilitation center. I researched our options, trying to find something we could afford. It was challenging. The rehabilitation care was going to be extremely expensive and this had emptied our pockets and purses already. The doctor said the rehab was important for Tommy and without it he would not be able to finish the healing process.

I did not know what to do at that point. So, I had to do what I knew to do, I went back to the Lord in prayer. If you pray in faith, God will answer your request. If you walk by faith, He will order your footsteps. I followed the doctor's directions and continued the search for a rehab facility, knowing this was all a part of the process.

The Lord laid it on three minister friends' hearts to put a letter together requesting financial help and they took it upon themselves to mail it out to all our friends and family. I am still so grateful for their act of generosity. People began to find out our need for rehab, and they began to give from everywhere.

God was so good, and *all* the money came in! God took care of every need. We needed healing for Tommy and it was happening! We needed finances for completion for rehab and God did it!

If you are one of the ones who gave, we would like to thank you at this time. If it was not for your help and obedience to the voice of the Lord, we do not know what we would have done. Again, thank you from the bottom of our hearts!

God is so faithful.

After several days of searching for a rehab facility and listening to the Lord for direction, Wednesday, March 14, we moved to the in-house rehab the hospital offered. I really wanted to go to this rehab because they were familiar with Tommy and what he had already been through. It all worked out beautifully and reminded me that God hears every request, all you have to do is ask and wait.

Be anxious for nothing, but in everything by prayer and supplication, with thanksgiving, let your requests be made known to God; and the peace of God, which surpasses all understanding, will guard your hearts and minds through Christ Jesus.

(Philippians 4:6-7 NKJV)

When we arrived at the rehab unit, they put us in a very tiny dark, private room that had a small window about twelve inches wide' and three feet long. Tommy was not able to rest in this room at all. He began to really struggle with the pain in his leg from the blood clot. The room was filled with so much depression. Tommy became very anxious and had a hard time finding peace. We prayed for peace in the room because we both felt so uncomfortable in it. We prayed the Lord would let a different room open up for us. Something had to change and change fast.

> *I continued to pray throughout the days that visitors came and went. Sometimes I could feel such warfare. It was heavier at night than in the day. I continued to push through in prayer by allowing the Spirit to pray through me to break whatever I was feeling.*

I never let my guard down in the spirit. I made sure I kept my spirit in tune with God, so I could recognize the enemy when he would try to push.

After three days had passed, on Saturday, March 17, we were told they were going to move Tommy to a different room. As far as I knew, no one had requested a new room. I was so excited! They moved him, and this time, into a suite. The room was four times larger than our previous room. This was definitely the favor of God working for our good!

Not only was this room into a private suite, there was a large window stretching the entire length of the wall. Tommy's new room was so large, I could put twelve to fifteen chairs in it, along with two hospital beds and still have plenty of room left for visitors. *What a difference God makes! Our prayers had been answered once again!* At night I was able to push the other bed in the room next to his, so they were side by side. For the first time since this process began I finally was able to lie down and sleep next to Tommy. That turned out to be a sweet gift from the Lord just for me.

That same night, when the nurse made the rounds to give Tommy his meds, I realized she did not give him his blood pressure medicine. I reminded her of it, but the nurse said the doctor had not ordered any. I knew this was wrong, so I requested they find out why. I also realized they had not given him his antibiotics for the sepsis as a precaution. Since I understood how serious sepsis was, I knew not to miss this medication. The devil will try any way he can stop the promise of God and I wanted to be sure I did not give him any leeway.

Hours later, another nurse came in to give him more meds, but again, no blood pressure medication was administered. Once again, I questioned them about it. Finally, after another hour, they brought it. I realized if I had not been there, attentive to his needs and watching, something bad could have happened because of these little slip-ups. The enemy would have loved to take Tommy out. The devil was still pushing against us. He would have loved to delay or discourage our progress or even end Tommy's life. I was not going to give him that opportunity, certainly not on my watch.

While he was in the rehab unit, I often played the same music throughout the day. Every day would start out the same. The nurses retaught him how to shave and shower. He learned how to bend over, pick up things, and walk up and down the stairs. He learned how to balance himself with a cane. They would talk to him about preaching and cooking, the things he loved to do. They asked what his plans were and what he was going to do in his future. It was so wonderful to hear him speak about his visions and dreams again. He answered, "I am going to make the devil pay for this!"

I continued to pray throughout the days that visitors came and went. Sometimes I could feel such warfare. It was heavier at night than in the day. I continued to push through in prayer by allowing the Spirit to pray through me to break whatever I was feeling. While we were in the in-house rehab, the days started running together. I could not keep them as distinctive as before. I was tired and had been in battle for weeks, but the joy of the Lord was still the strength from which I drew.

One evening while praying in the middle of the night, I felt so much torment and evil around us. I turned to prayer again, hard and vigorously while trying to keep quiet. About thirty minutes into intercession, a male nurse from Africa came into the room. He was the night nurse *that happened* (I believe nothing just happens) to be assigned to Tommy. He saw on Tommy's chart that he was a pastor. He shared with me that he believed in miracles and he had seen many and asked if he could pray for Tommy. We both told him, "Yes, please do."

When he opened his mouth and began to pray, he took authority and dominion over the attack of the devil. At that very moment you could feel such a vibration in the atmosphere of the room. Things began to shift. Together, we were commanding, decreeing and declaring over Tommy's healing and for his future. The torment lifted! The authority was very strong. It was so powerful, God set up an agent of His to bring in someone who could agree with us and provide extra authority and covering over my husband that night. When you know your authority, it changes things when you pray. The devil realizes you know who you are in God. I will never forget that man of God!

God is so mindful of us.

God is mindful of you, too.

He will order your footsteps even when you are not physically able. God will order favor to come to you and send to you those who can help you get your miracle.

I began to share with the nurse all we had been through, and he explained this particular in-house rehab used to be an insane asylum. *Wow, did that answer a lot of questions I had running around in my mind!*

After prayer and worship, just as before, the nurses would come into our room and share how peaceful and different our room was from everyone else's. The power of prayer is amazing. It pushed back the darkness of agony and pain, not just in our room, but in others as well.

Thank God Tommy's physical development was progressing well even though his right arm and leg were still not as strong as the rest of his body. Particularly, his right leg was just a little slower than the left. But through time and working in the rehab, the right arm and leg were almost the same strength as the left.

Just because there is not any physical sign of an instant

change, does not mean God has left you to figure out the rest on your own. I recall reading the story of a blind man in the Gospels, Mark 8:24-26 where Jesus prayed for a man and his eyesight was not healed immediately. When he opened his eyes to see, at that time, his eyes were in the beginning process of healing. His report to Jesus was, I see men as trees. So, Jesus prayed again, and the man's eyes were completely made whole.

Remember, healing is a process, but a miracle is instant! Sometimes the healing power of God is gradual, and we have to keep our eyes on Him and trust He will finish the work He started.

Tommy was having problems with short-term memory, but his cognitive skills were great, as with everything else. He even knew who everyone was now! Progress demands patience and while I am still working on that area of my life, I have learned to lean on the Lord and know He is patient with me as well.

By March 18, Tommy started remembering things he did throughout the day, which turned out to be very good progress. He sang and worshiped *all* the time. Moment by moment, day by day, I could see him changing. The Holy Spirit kept him while his flesh was weak, but now his flesh was becoming stronger.

The balancing of his spirit and his flesh was becoming normal again. He started facing emotional and spiritual inner war that was different from before. Tommy's faith had to stand back up within him. It was like watching a child grow all over again.

The doctors came and took the staples out of his head from surgery. Tommy would get cloudy on some days and on other days he would be better. I did not know it at that time, but I would continue to see those kinds of days for the next nine and half years as we walked through the healing process together. It was not fun, but God's grace is sufficient.

Not only was his body healing back together, but his thoughts and his emotions as well.

You have to learn to keep your mind thinking on the things of the Lord (Philippians 4:8-11). Think on who He is and what He can and will do. Remember, there is nothing too hard for Him and He is the miracle worker. You control your thoughts not your thoughts control you. You must keep the good fight of faith (1 Timothy 6:12). Remember, a good fight is not how hard the battle is, but the one you win. This is such an answer to prayer in receiving what you are praying and believing.

Finally, brethren, whatever things are true, whatever things are noble, whatever things are just, whatever things are pure, whatever things are lovely, whatever things are of good report, if there is any virtue and if there is anything praiseworthy—meditate on these things. The things which you learned and received and heard and saw in me, these do, and the God of peace will be with you.

(Philippians 4:8-9 NKJV)

Fight the good fight of the faith; lay hold of the eternal life to which you were summoned and [for which] you confessed the good confession [of faith] before many witnesses.

(1 Timothy 6:12 Amplified)

The doctors were so amazed; everyone in the hospital was talking about him. He was the talk of the town! There were nurses from all over the hospital who would come in to see him because they could not believe he was still alive and operating normally on "so many fronts."

Tommy's vision was still not as it should be. The eye could see, but the brain did not connect the vision with the eye. The peripheral vision of the right eye was not working correctly as well as the lower peripheral vision which caused him much struggle to see clearly. He kept having blurred vision and distorted images. He remained dizzy for a while, but we both would speak the Bible scriptures together and believe God was not through with him. If He was, He would have taken Tommy when He had the opportunity. As therapy continued, his right arm and leg became so much stronger, but Tommy had been in the recovery bed for so long that the pain from the blood clot was still an issue. It would be so painful at times it made it difficult for Tommy to walk during therapy. Eventually, the pain subsided. He had been walking with a walker, but by the time we left rehab, he was just using a cane.

Chapter 21

✹

He Turned It
Karen

While standing in Tommy's room on March 22, it became obvious that the healing power of God returned in a very strong way. This is the room where Tommy says he "woke up," which is the only way he can describe it.

He says his feelings became aware of his natural surroundings. He went from being in a heavenly realm to knowing he was now in a hospital from having brain surgery. After waking up from a deep peaceful sleep, he realized his life had been in great jeopardy. He was aware he was no longer in that peaceful place he just experienced, but now surrounded with chaos. He now felt the change from the peaceful atmosphere he was in, to the harshness of reality in our confusing world. He knew he was back in his earthly home.

He does remember one room in CCU for a moment, but that is all. This is the place where his memory always goes back to and he begins to remember more.

After staying ten days at the in-house rehab, the medical team now wanted Tommy to go to an outpatient rehab. What progress!

The Lord opened a door right away for Tommy to go to a special rehabilitation facility. This facility is one of the very few places that have a special outpatient rehab program for patients recovering from brain trauma. Not only did he get to go, but it was also paid for *in full*!

On Friday March 30, we left the in-house rehab. Tommy left rehab only needing three medications. That was another major miracle and to look back at what God did is incredibly sweet and amazing. That Sunday, he was able to go to church for the first time since the journey began and finally to be in worship service with everyone again.

I did not know at that time we would have another eleven years of healing. I never thought, *how long will this take?* I never thought, *will he ever be completely healed?* I just knew, *if God brought us this far, He would take us all the way.*

The following Monday, Tommy started outpatient rehab. The therapists worked him through various exercises. They had him walk on a treadmill and he had to stand on a ball while balancing himself. He then would jump and throw the ball in the air and then catch it. *I cannot even do that, but he did it.* He had to walk on a balance beams and he would have to do puzzles, build models, and other things that would help his cognitive reasoning. All these things helped his brain recover, but it made him very tired.

Tommy started driving again in April 2007. The doctor was shocked that he could drive. Remember, Tommy was supposed to be a vegetable for the rest of his life! Several years later, Tommy leaned over to me and asked me the question, "If I had been a vegetable, which one do you think I would have turned out to be?" Of course I told him *I have no clue* and we both laughed!

That same month, he was released from the outpatient rehab center and they explained to me, after brain surgery, the brain would continue to heal, and the cognitive skills would become better. It was going to take time, but I did not care at all. He is alive by the grace of God!

They handed me a chart that showed the progression of brain healing. The chart was a picture of a graph going up a page like the side of a mountain. They explained while Tommy traveled up the mountain, there would be a notch or drop in the graph. Each notch or drop represented one bad day or several difficult days. When either of these would happen, he would have to rest and recoup to give his brain a chance to heal while he rested.

When he would come out of the notch or drop in the graph, he would be better than before. Here we go, climbing the hill and facing the bad days and experiencing the better days. We just kept on traveling up our mountain of life. By the help of God and others, we never stopped climbing.

They explained to me that I would definitely see the differences in him. At first when he was released, I could not tell the difference between good days and bad days. They all were bad, but I *refused* to focus on them. I only *saw him healed*.

When he had a bad day, I did not act differently from when he had a good day. I was determined that God had begun a good work in him and He would completely finish what He had started out to do! I just believed.

"Being confident of this very thing, that
He who has begun a good work in you will complete
it until the day of Jesus Christ."
(Philippians 6:1 KJV)

Tommy began to preach a little here and there on Sundays. He held his first revival meeting that lasted an entire week, April 2007, in a little West Texas town.

Tommy drove us six and a half hours to our first meeting for our friends. He was not able to walk up and down the stairs on the platform unless he had help and he moved very slowly.

However, when he began to preach, he jumped up and down, and went up and down those stairs without a thought. He never struggled while he preached. It was amazing how the anointing worked. The presence of God would come on him and he would be normal in his walking and preaching skills. God is so powerful! When Tommy was through preaching he would need help coming off the platform again.

It was like a "God blanket" would be thrown over him while he ministered, and then when he was finished, the blanket was removed. As long as the blanket was on him, he could do what was impossible for him alone, but the moment the blanket was removed, he went right back to the same man who had just come out of the hospital.

Brain surgery patients require a lot of sleep to help the brain continue its healing process. Tommy would sleep at least fifteen hours a day. He would sleep and then get up and go preach each night. It was amazing to watch the healing that came from being in the anointing. The anointing brings healing. In fact, scripture says the anointing is the only thing that can break the yoke.

*It shall come to pass in that day
That his burden will be taken away from your shoulder,
And his yoke from your neck, And the yoke will be destroyed because of the anointing oil*

(Isaiah 10:27 NKJV)

I never treated Tommy as if he had had brain surgery or as if he was limited. I treated him as if nothing had ever happened. I look back and really believe that if I had pampered the struggle he was having, he would have stayed in the struggle. I never gave attention to what had happened, just to the miracle we had.

In July we flew to Colorado to preach our second meeting at Abundant Life Church for our dear friends, Pastor Rick and Marietta Walls. We stayed there for three weeks. When Tommy would step up to take the microphone to preach, you could never tell he was struggling at all. The Spirit of the Lord would come all over him, and he would become strong just like in the past.

The Spirit of God is so alive and real. This is why it is important to let your inner-man really be filled with all the fullness of God. When you have filled yourself with Jesus, it is Him that will come out of you. He will come out of your walk, talk and even your testimony. You are living proof that Jesus is everything the Bible says about Him. Jesus is ALIVE!

As time passed, Tommy would continue to have good days and bad days. On the bad days, he would struggle so hard trying to think normally and just trying to function. During these days, he could not do much. He would get so frustrated because he could not do what he wanted to do. He tried once to climb a stepladder and he could not do it. Simple things like that would make him feel stupid and then he would fight insecurities. As the months passed, he would continue to try going up the ladder again and again. Eventually, he could make it up a few steps.

The doctor put him on a drug called Keppra. The side effects from that drug were very hard for both of us to live with. The side effects of the medicine and the brain trying to process everything was very difficult for him to handle at times. He would battle with his emotions through his daily routine. There were a couple of times we attempted go to the mall and had to turn back around and leave. He could not handle the people walking toward him. He could not process what was really happening; it would become very overwhelming for him.

Chapter 22

Possessing My Authority
Karen

We were driving home one day and Tommy's emotions were warring against him. I did not realize it was the Keppra causing these problems. It was more than he could handle. He became so angry, he felt like he could not take it anymore. I began to pray and plead the blood of Jesus over him and me. I was well aware the situation was becoming very serious and intense.

At that moment, the Spirit of God on the inside of Tommy compelled him to exit and pull over. I was praying, believing God to protect us. He crossed four lanes of one of the busiest interstates in Texas, I-75 in Dallas. He pulled into a parking lot, got out, and started walking across an open field. At that moment, I knew the battle had shifted one more time, so I went into prayer again. After the drug had subsided, he calmed down and I drove over to where he had walked. I picked him up and I drove us back home. That was the only time something that drastic happened. I know it was resolved because of prayer.

> *The Spirit of God on the inside of Tommy compelled him to exit and pull over...At that moment, I knew the battle had shifted one more time, so I went into prayer again.*

You must learn to shift with the battle. We were no longer

fighting for life on the operating table, but we were fighting to regain strength in the mind from those surgeries. You have to recognize when the shift happens, so your prayer life can shift along with it.

I realized I had to stay on guard to protect him from the enemy who was still trying to destroy not only him, but me and our son as well. I had fought too hard and too long to allow anything to happen now. I was determined to keep myself in the right mindset with God so I could help Tommy be completely free from the mental attacks.

At first, he had more bad days than good. Over time, I watched him mend through a long process, and finally he began to have more good days than bad. As we crossed over into one year from brain surgery, things were changing. He was becoming more and more healed. He was becoming stronger.

I learned something very valuable walking through this process that I hope you gather from our experience. It is important that you learn *how to pray*. Not just pray a simple religious prayer, but know how to access the heart of God, and eventually see the results you are needing.

As I would see these bad days come on him, I would begin to go into spiritual warfare. I would pray under my breath quickly and quietly, but with *great authority! I meant it!* It did not matter where I was. If I was at the store among a group of people, I would begin to pray and bind the enemy's stronghold. No one knew what I was doing, but I always knew the devil sure did. I not only meant what I prayed, but I BELIEVED what I prayed.

Remember, faith is knowing. Even when we were going through it at that very moment, I knew the enemy was defeated. I told the enemy to stop using Tommy's weakness of the flesh against him.

I would strongly *command* the enemy to get off of his mind and get out of his emotions! Within thirty minutes or so, I would see Tommy getting better, and eventually I would begin to see a change in him. Through time, I would see the attacks coming and I would start praying to stop the attack before it became too strong. *I had to be consistently alert and strong.* I was ready for these moments of control to leave him once and for all. Instead, *Tommy* finally got to where he would control his *own* life.

PRAYER WORKS!

I constantly pushed to keep him in the pulpit preaching the Word. I knew the anointing was where Gods' healing and sustaining power was. The anointing brings complete healing.

Keppra is a drug that is used to prevent seizures. A few of the side effects of this drug are dizziness, restlessness, depression, loss of memory, lack of coordination, mood changes, anxiousness, irritability, and thoughts of suicide. He wrestled with most of these side effects, which caused it to be very difficult for him to have a normal life. He was miserable. His struggles from this drug was very hard for him and me.

On March 3, 2008, at 5:30 a.m. in the morning, Tommy was sound asleep in bed.

Suddenly, he sat straight up in bed and said, "The Lord just spoke to me in my sleep"

Trying hard to wake up to see what was going on I asked, "What did He say?"

Tommy shared that the Lord told him to stop Keppra and not take it anymore, even though the doctors had warned me previously not to let him come off Keppra cold turkey. Seizures and even death can result from suddenly stopping Keppra; patients must be under a doctor's super-vision while tapering off this medicine. Tommy had *The Great Physician* telling him to stop taking it.

From that day on, he never took another pill. God completely delivered him from the side effects and all that comes from the drug. It truly was a miracle! Please note: I do *not* recommend this to anyone without a doctor's permission. This is simply what we chose to do in our situation.

> *By this time, we had used up all our savings and gone through financial struggles...We continued to preach and pray for people, believing God for miracles. I do not know how, but in April 2012, we were able to purchase our very first home.*

Tommy kept changing and growing. He still dealt with a lot

of emotions, but as he healed, he was more and more able to keep those emotions from ruling him.

In December 2011, we were at my parents' home in Florida and we had all gone shopping. Tommy was still fighting good days and bad days at the time. I would still pray over him under my breath with *great authority and power*, but I never let myself get tired of defeating the enemy. I was going to have a miracle. It worked and every time he would get better. It was a strong fight, it was hard to break, but with God's intervention we made it.

When we got in the car to leave, Tommy asked my father to pray for him. Tommy said he actually physically felt something being pulled off of the back of his head, like the suction of a vacuum. It was a breakthrough moment and he has felt different ever since.

In February 2012, Tommy was preaching another revival and I had to leave town for a couple of weeks. After I returned, there was such a change in him. I knew the war was over, the struggle had ended, and he was closer to being *completely healed!!*

He shared with me that there were just a few more times he had felt "cloudy" as he called it, but it would leave quickly.

By this time, we had used up all our savings and gone through financial struggles. We had to keep our trust in God and our mind on Him. Our electricity was turned off twice, our water service was turned off three times, but we kept pushing. Despite all we went through, God never failed. We went through such a struggle, even though we hated it, we had to go on food stamps for a short while. We never allowed ourselves to lose our joy and the vision for the future. We knew we were not going to stay there for very long and we did not.

We continued to preach and pray for people, believing God for miracles. I do not know how, but in April 2012, we were able to purchase our very first home. It is a beautiful two-story rock and brick home of almost three thousand square feet. We now own one of the largest lots in our neighborhood. We have rose bushes and plants of all kinds. It is just beautiful! We do not know how that happened, "but God."

By June 2012, his memory had gotten better and better until it was better than mine. What a sweet, wonderful Jesus we serve! He truly is a healer and a peace-giver. He has given us the answer to everything and if we want it, it is up to us to walk in it!

Without the scar Tommy has on the top of his head from the surgery, you would never know anything had ever happened.

Chapter 23

Authentic Miracle

Karen

There is no doubt God has given us a miracle.

Today, in Tommy's head, there is a dark hole where they removed the bleed from his brain. They did not remove any of the brain, but the entire nine-centimeter circumference (about the size of a medium potato) where there *was* a part of the brain, has died because it was touched by the blood. Our doctor explained to us why. Imagine the area of the brain as if it were cotton candy. If you touch cotton candy with your mouth, it evaporates. This is exactly what has happened in Tommy's brain. On the portion of where the blood touched his brain, there is literally, a hollow spot in his head.

The doctors are shocked Tommy can drive. They are astounded he stopped Keppra and has no seizures. They do not understand why he is functioning like a normal man today. There is no medical reasoning and no scientific answers.

One doctor recently said, "I just want to stare at you. I cannot believe you are alive."

WE CAN!

God is always faithful. He will never leave us or forsake us.

When you are given a bad report from the doctor, I am not saying for you to ignore the report given to you, but to instead recognize you have a choice. What you choose to do with the report you have been given, is up to you. Whose report will you believe? Keep your prayer life going and commit to your relationship with God. Grow your faith, feed your faith. Faith comes by hearing the Word (Romans 10:17). This will have you in the right place when any report given to you may breed fear. Faith will override any doubt, fear, or worry.

When you do these things, you are preparing yourself for whatever life brings. You will respond differently, think differently, and know differently. It will change your destiny.

Through the darkest hours you face, there is a hope for tomorrow. The trials you go through do not necessarily mean it is over for you. Instead they can be doors to the goodness of God in your life, doors that bring greater anointing, power, and authority in Christ Jesus.

Know your rights as a child of God in the Kingdom. There is a promise for your future. Connect your faith with His promises. Always remember, in Him, all things really are possible -- this side of Heaven.

Shalom to you all in Christ's name, Amen!

Thank you, Jesus, for all you have done!

What a healer and a miracle-worker you are!!!

"Let your conduct be without covetousness;

be content with such things as you have. For He Himself

has said, "I will never leave you nor forsake you."

(Hebrews 13:5 KJV)

"I have been young and now am old;

Yet I have not seen the righteous forsake,

Nor his descendants begging bread."

(Psalm 37:25 KJV)

"I have begun a good work in you

and I will finish what I have started."

(Philippians 1:6 KJV)

Chapter 24

It is Your Turn

If you hold onto the promises of God for your life, you will see them fulfilled. When others say it is impossible, you cannot give up. When everything around you screams the worst is going to happen, you cannot give up.

1. **You must let Jesus be everything in your life and accept Him as your Savior.**

Considering yourself a "good person" is not enough. *For all have sinned and come short of the Glory of God.* Realize being a good person is not enough to be with Him in Heaven (Romans 3:23, Romans 3:10, Romans 5:12). We must recognize we were born into sin and we have to believe that Jesus died for those sins (Romans 6:23). Remember, He loves you so much that no matter what you have done, He will forgive you of those sins (Romans 5:8). How can I be saved? (Romans 10:9-10). Now that you have accepted Him, what do you do next? (Romans 10:17). You can know He heard you by reading Romans 10:17. It is not if He loves you enough, but do you love Him enough?

For all have sinned and fall short of the glory of God.
(Romans 3:23 NKJV)

"There is none righteous, no, not one;"
(Romans 3:10 NKJV)

Therefore, just as through one man sin

entered the world and death through sin, and thus death

spread to all men, because all sinned.

(Romans 5:12 NKJV)

For the wages of sin [is] death,

but the gift of God [is] eternal life in Christ

Jesus our Lord.

(Romans 6:23 NKJV)

But God demonstrates His own love

toward us, in that while we were still sinners,

Christ died for us.

(Romans 5:8 NKJV)

*"that if you confess with your mouth
the Lord Jesus and believe in your heart that God has raised
Him from the dead, you will be saved. For with the
heart one believes unto righteousness, and with
the mouth confession is made unto salvation"
(Romans 10:9-10 NKJV)*

For *"whoever calls on the
name of the LORD shall be saved."
(Romans 10:13 NKJV)*

2. *You must stay in the Word and pray.*

Take time out of each day to talk to the Lord and read His word. Know the Word of God is powerful, and when you use it, it works.

*"So then faith comes by hearing,
and hearing by the Word of God."
(Romans 10:17 KJV)*

*"Then you will call upon me and come
and pray to me, and I will hear you. You will
seek me and find me, when you seek me with all
your heart. I will be found by you, declares the LORD, and I will
restore your fortunes and gather you from all the nations and
all the places where I have driven you, declares
the LORD, and I will bring you back to the place
from which I sent you into exile."
(Jeremiah 29:12-14)*

*"Ask, and it will be given to you; seek, and you
will find; knock, and it will be opened to you. For everyone who
asks receives, and the one who seeks finds, and to the
one who knocks it will be opened."
(Matthew 7:7-8 NKJV)*

"But seek first the kingdom of God
and his righteousness, and all these things
will be added to you."
(Matthew 6:33 NKJV)

"You will seek me and find me, when you
seek me with all your heart."
(Jeremiah 29:13 NKJV)

"By faith in the name of Jesus, this man whom
you see" and know was made strong. It is Jesus' name
and the faith that comes through him that has
completely healed him, as you can all"
(Acts 3:16 NKJV)

"Call to Me, and I will answer you, and show you great
and mighty things, which you do not know"
(Jeremiah 33:3 NKJV)

3. You must keep God as the most important thing in your life.

Make sure you put Him first in all you do. Inquire of Him on any decision you make.

So they said to him, "Please inquire of God,
that we may know whether the journey on which we go will be
prosperous." And the priest said to them, "Go in peace. The
presence of the Lord be with you on your way."
(Judges 18:5-6 NKJV)

In all your ways acknowledge Him,
And He shall direct your paths.
(Proverbs 3:6 NKJV)

> *"But seek first the kingdom of God*
> *and his righteousness, and all these things*
> *will be added to you."*
> *(Matthew 6:33 NKJV)*

> *"Be anxious for nothing, but in*
> *Everything by prayer and supplication,*
> *with thanksgiving, let your requests be made*
> *known to God; and the peace of God, which*
> *surpasses all understanding, will guard your hearts*
> *and minds through Christ Jesus."*
> *(Philippians 4:6-7 NKJV)*

4. **You must control your thoughts that would like to overtake you with doubt and fear by keeping your mind stayed on Him.**

You must apply the Word that says, *take every thought captive*. Keep your mind fixed on His promise. Do not allow your mind to wander in any way.

"And do not be conformed to this world,
but be transformed by the renewing of your mind,
that you may prove what is that good
and acceptable and perfect will of God."
(Romans 12:2 NKJV)

"And whatever things you ask in prayer,
believing, you will receive."
(Matthew 21:22 NKJV)

'And the LORD, He is the One who goes
before you. He will be with you, He will not leave you nor
forsake you; do not fear nor be dismayed."
(Deuteronomy 31:8 NKJV)

> *"Casting down imaginations, and every high thing*
> *That exalts itself against the knowledge of God, and bringing*
> *into captivity every thought to the obedience of Christ;"*
> *(2 Corinthians 10:5 KJV)*

5. Meditate on Him and His Word.

First, meditate on the Word. Do not just read it, but let it speak to you. Absorb it into your mind until your subconscious must bring it up and you repeat it (aloud) when you need it the most.

> *"This Book of the Law shall not depart from*
> *your mouth, but you shall meditate in it day and night,*
> *that you may observe to do according to all that is written in it.*
> *For then you will make your way prosperous,*
> *and then you will have good success."*
> *(Joshua 1:8 NKJV)*

"May my meditation be sweet to Him;

I will be glad in the LORD."

(Psalm 104:34 NKJV)

"I will meditate on Your precepts,

And contemplate Your ways.

(Psalm 119:15 KNJV)

6. He MUST be the center of your life.

There is nothing more important than allowing Jesus to lead you and guide you. As you make Him the center of your life, He will show you great and mighty things you do not know.

But seek first the kingdom of God
and his righteousness, and all these
things will be added to you.
(Matthew 6:33 NKJV)

He must increase, but I [must] decrease.

(John 3:30 NKJV)

You must have a relationship with Jesus, He loves you more than you know. Your relationship with Him will become very personal as you pursue Him by praying and reading His Word and He will move for you as you grow in Him.

I do not mean for you to ignore the report that has been given to you, but recognize you have a choice. We all have a choice. What you choose to do with the report you have been given is up to you. Whose report will you believe?

Keep your prayer life going as well as your relationship with God. I want to encourage you to feed your faith, because faith comes by hearing the Word (Romans 10:17). In my experience I have found when I have received a negative report of any kind, I turn to the Lord in prayer and His Words of promise. Find for yourself a scripture that you connect with and believe the report that brings you hope in the midst of trouble. Having this promise makes you feel hopeful and hope places you in the right place for a miracle. When bad reports are given, there is a chance that fear will try to overwhelm you, but have faith in God. Faith will override any doubt, fear, or worry.

When you do these things, you are preparing yourself for whatever life throws your way. I believe you will respond differently, think differently, and your results become what God has promised you. It will change your destiny.

Through the darkest hours you face, there is a hope for tomorrow. The trials you go through do not necessarily mean it is over for you; instead they can be doors to the blessings of God in your life. Doors that bring greater anointing, power, and authority in Christ Jesus.

Know your rights as a child of God in the Kingdom and believe that every promise will be fulfilled in your future. Connect your faith with His promises and always remember, in Him, all things really are possible this side of Heaven.

Shalom to you all in Christ's name, Amen!

Thank you, Jesus, for all you have done!

What a healer and a miracle-worker you are!!!

*"I have begun a good work in you
and I will finish what I have started."*

(Philippians 1:6 KJV)

Medical Side and Report

Todd Clinard

Let me begin by saying that my wife and I have been in the medical field in one capacity or another for most of our careers. I was a corpsman in the US Navy where I was trained as a paramedic/ER nurse. After being discharged, I then attended and graduated from college and became a registered nurse.

Since then I have worked in the intensive care unit, preoperative unit, post-anesthesia care unit (recovery room), and the operating room. My wife has been working in the operating room for more than twenty years now and is currently the Chief Nursing Officer at one of Texas main health hospital.

When God anoints a medically trained mind, it is at times a struggle for your faith, and a revelation of the wonder and power of the One True God.

Because the mind is trained to see what is normal: meaning, how the body is programmed to react to sickness, disease, cancer, and other infirmities. It is an attack on your faith early in your ministry when you see the reality and impossibility of the medical circumstances in the people before you in a church service and knowing in the back of your mind that you have seen these circumstances have poor outcomes in your workplace.

However, you must stand firm in your faith knowing what God's Word says about the frailty of sickness and disease considering the healing power of Jesus...and you must remind yourself it is the *prayer of faith* that heals the sick.

There is also another side to that coin. When you see there is absolutely no way the body could heal itself that quickly or efficiently, no reason why this person who has been afflicted with cancer, heart disease, etc., is now walking around disease-free within one day or week after they received prayer, then it is all the more miraculous to you than to most anyone else because you know there is no way this outcome could be anything but a pure miracle from God.

On the night we were to begin our first revival in our first storefront, my wife and I were at home getting ready for service when Pastor Karen called telling me Pastor was not feeling right. She told me he had a horrible headache, was dizzy, and she had given him some ibuprofen and had him lay down for a while, but his headache was getting worse. In addition to that, he was beginning to lose his right-sided vision in both eyes.

It was the latter that alarmed me, and I instructed her to put him in the car and immediately take him to the emergency room at the hospital where my wife and I worked at the time. I went on to church to take care of the service for the night, despite knowing from my experience his situation could in fact be very severe.

I walked into the service that night not knowing exactly how I was going to proceed but trusting God would lead the way. When I opened the service, the Lord spoke to me and had me turn the service into a prayer meeting. I then gave everyone a summary of what had happened to their pastor and told them we needed to touch God on his behalf that night.

After we had interceded and prayed for some time, I dismissed everyone, and my wife and I drove to the hospital. We found when we arrived that my gut feeling before service was absolutely correct. While we were in service, a barrage of tests had been performed, only to discover he had a bleed on his brain that had grown to the size of a tangerine on the CT scan...not the good news we wanted to hear.

Pastor was not very coherent, and barely recognized my voice when I arrived. He still did not have vision on his right side before he became incoherent, and his right side had become very weak.

The symptoms all pointed to the severity of the bleed in his brain from an aneurysm (a weak spot in an artery), which caused a serious condition, a subdural hematoma, and simply did not look favorable at all.

I was very happy to see the neurosurgeon on call that night was the one neurosurgeon I would want to operate on me or any of my family members. He had authored books on neurosurgery and had two PhD's.

This was a very intelligent man to say the least. Pastor was admitted to the ICU, and the doctor said it looked like the bleeding had stopped for now. It was best to see if the body would absorb the clot verses opening the skull and exposing him to brain surgery.

He would be kept under observation for the night. As we stood there listening to him talk to us and the family about his observations and his plans, he also said, according to his experience, his outcome was bleak at best. "He will never be the same," he said. He did not know how right he was.

Early the next morning, as my wife and I were on our way to the hospital, Pastor Karen called me in a panic. She told me everyone was moving around very hurriedly and asking her to sign papers.

When I finally got her to tell me what the nurses had said to her, my stomach sank. When the brain experiences dangerous levels of swelling and pressure, it causes the pupils of the eyes to react in a very specific way. One pupil dilates all the way, and the other closes to a pinpoint. He was bleeding again. The papers they were asking her to sign were consents and documents to take him into surgery to perform a craniotomy to evacuate the blood clot and to stop the bleeding.

If this was not done quickly, he would die very soon. We arrived at the unit about the same time as the neurosurgeon. He was polite and gentle, but bluntly honest about the severity of the situation, and the bleak outlook ahead of him if he even makes it out of surgery alive.

Let me now explain the severity of a bleed in the brain, (a subdural hematoma, a leaking aneurysm) and the effects of subjecting a person to brain surgery. The brain is a very fragile organ, not completely understood by medical science.

Anytime blood escapes from the vessels and collects in the surrounding brain tissue, it kills brain cells. It also causes pressure on the brain tissue by leaking excess blood into an enclosed area. If you could inflate a balloon inside a jar, and then inject fluid between the balloon and the jar, the balloon will become compressed because there is not room for the excess fluid within the jar. This is what happens when a blood vessel ruptures inside the brain. The tissue of the brain is much softer than the skull that surrounds it, so naturally, the brain will compress before the skull expands. This pressure is detrimental to the brain tissue, as is the pooling blood on the tissue, as both cause irreparable damage to the brain.

The area of the brain that has been affected by the bleed determines what part of the body will be affected by the damage of those particular brain cells. If you survive the bleed itself (which many do not) to make it into surgery, most patients have permanent brain damage. Parts of their memory are blotted out, they may not be able to walk the same or at all, speech may be different, motor functions are sometimes impaired, eyesight and/or hearing may be lost, and most every patient has trouble with cognitive functioning. This is the ability to problem solve.

Most things these patients struggle with are decisions or circumstances that everyone deals with 100 times a day with hardly any thought at all. It is usually because the circuits of normal thought patterns are broken. Therefore, because the processes of normal thought are broken, the person cannot transition to another solution within their mind to solve a simple matter and are essentially stuck not knowing what to do next.

Some have to learn to walk again, how to perform simple motor functions, how to feed themselves, how to dress themselves, and some patients never recover at all.

Now, here is where my medical knowledge of the situation can test my faith, but also show the ways in which God is involved that no one else is able to comprehend. Right before they were about to roll him down to the OR, the ICU nurse came out and said to my wife and myself, "OK, it is a little strange, but for some reason his pupils have normalized." This made my wife and I raise an eyebrow. That would not normally occur unless the pressure has subsided. Ok God, what are you doing?

Since my wife and I worked at this facility, we knew the staff involved in the surgery. We were told by the OR nurse who was in the surgery that when they had opened the skull to evacuate the clot, (and I apologize if this is graphic for some) the pressure was so high inside his skull that blood shot across the room. She said in all her years of working in brain surgery she had never seen pressure that severe on a patient. So, if the pressure was that intense, why did his pupils normalize on the way down to the OR as if the pressure had subsided?

I honestly was not worried. At this point, especially because his pupils normalized, I knew God was involved, and He was going to carry Pastor through this entirely. I knew it even when the surgeon came out and told us he would be doing good to walk well again, that he would absolutely never preach again, never play the piano and sing again and at best all we could expect was for him to be little more than a vegetable, barely able to function in society.

And true to what we had seen during our careers, the following week in the hospital went exactly as expected from a medical standpoint. He did not recognize a lot of people at times. Some days he did not recognize anyone but his wife. He thought my wife was Martha Stewart. He thought he was other places, and really had a zombie-like expression; his countenance was sluggish and blank. He had little or no facial expression.

At the end of the week, he started bleeding again, to make a bad situation worse. Again, they rushed him down to surgery. Unknown to us or the medical staff at the time, he had also developed a urinary tract infection that week. When they got him down to the OR suite, his condition and his vital signs all pointed to, once again, a very bleak outcome. In fact, it was worse than it was a week ago before the first craniotomy. It was so bad the surgeon told everyone in the OR they could not waste any time whatsoever, because he was probably going to die, and he did not think he could survive the anesthesia, much less the surgery itself.

Well, he did survive the surgery, but because his body's defenses were already in a compromised state, he was not able to fight off the infection, and he became septic. A septic infection is an infection that has spread into the bloodstream, affecting all organs. A staggering 80% of patients who develop septic shock die *even with treatment.* So, here he was, in the ICU recovering from a second craniotomy within ten days, and he has now gone septic. When my wife and I walked into his room, my faith began to crumble.

For the first time since this all had started, I thought he was going to die. For the first time I began to question God about what He was doing.

He was on the ventilator, unable to breathe on his own. His blood pressure was 50/20, and he was on two of the strongest

IV medications for raising blood pressure, both at the same time. His kidneys had shut down, his liver function tests showed his liver was shutting down. He was in multi-organ failure.

Most patients have a long hard road trying to recover from sepsis alone, much less the added two brain surgeries within ten days. He had a gray, what we call in the medical field "dusky" appearance. Whenever someone is getting ready to die, their skin becomes a grayish color (called dusky) and their eyes seem to sink in a little. I had seen this many times before, but this time it was different. I was watching my friend die in front of my very eyes.

When we came out of the unit, into the waiting room, we must have had a look of horror on our faces. Two of his friends, who were pastors, came up to us and said, "It is really bad, is not it? He is really in bad shape, isn't he?" Not wanting to alarm them or his family, I just told them the situation was very severe and we all really need to pray for him.

About that time, his wife, who was across the room in a small group and could not hear me speaking with them, stood up and said, "I do not know what is going on right now, but I really feel like we need to pray right now." So, a group of us found a remote hallway around the corner from the waiting room, and we started praying (as Pastor would have put it; "like our hair was on fire").

We all prayed so hard and so intensely that we scared some of the hospital staff that were trying to come down the hallway. They just stopped and looked at us, and then turned around and went the other way!

The next morning, we got the report that "somehow" he turned completely around. His color came back, his blood pressure came back. So much so that they had to take him off the IV blood pressure medications he was on just eight hours earlier. His kidneys were functioning, and his liver function tests had come back up to normal.

For my wife and I, there was no doubt in our minds that God had intervened. Medically speaking, I have seen too many people die in that situation, and they definitely do not turn around so quickly.

Over the next weeks and months, we watched him slowly make his way back. We saw him recover day after day, week after week, month after month, past the point the doctors had initially said he would progress.

I remember him coming back from one of the last visits to the neurosurgeon's office, a month or so after he got out of the hospital. He told me the doctor just sat and stared at him. He asked me about it, and I told him the surgeon was probably trying to figure out why and how he was still alive and sitting in front of him.

I have watched God heal him completely. There are little things here and there I see that, honestly, are so minuscule and happen so infrequently that no one notices but me, which are leftover glitches that God has not completely healed yet. He sings, plays the piano, the organ, and preaches like never before.

He has an incredible testimony. That neurosurgeon had one thing correct: he will definitely never be the same!

PICTURES OF SURGERY

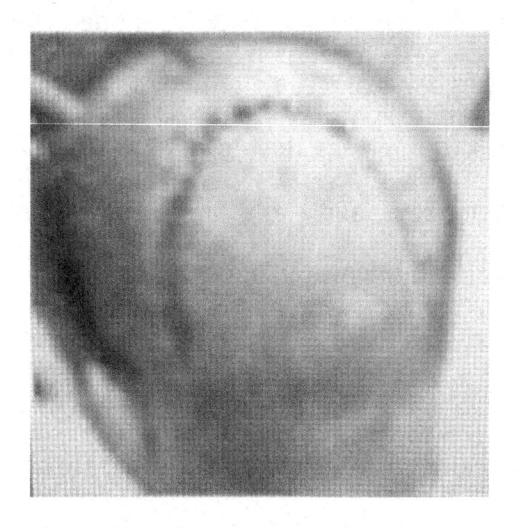

The large incision in the shape of a horseshoe on the Back left of his head which was closed with staples. He Still has the scar today of his testimony!

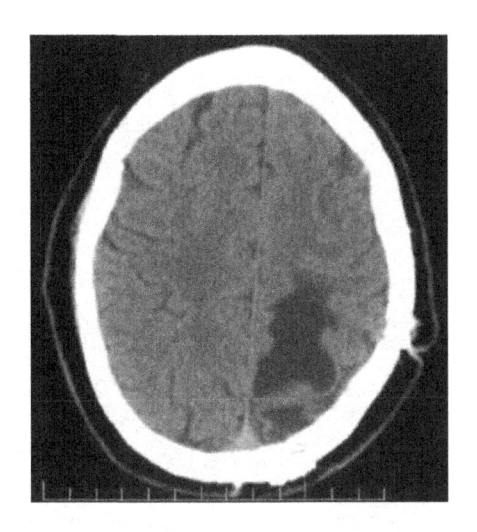

*2 pictures of the MRI where the blood touched the brain

which caused a hole in the brain.

Still there today.*

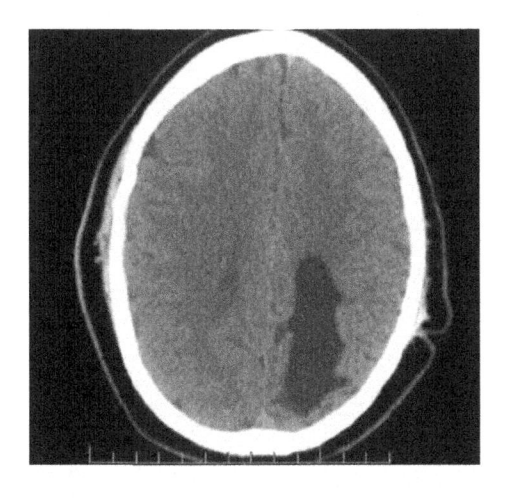

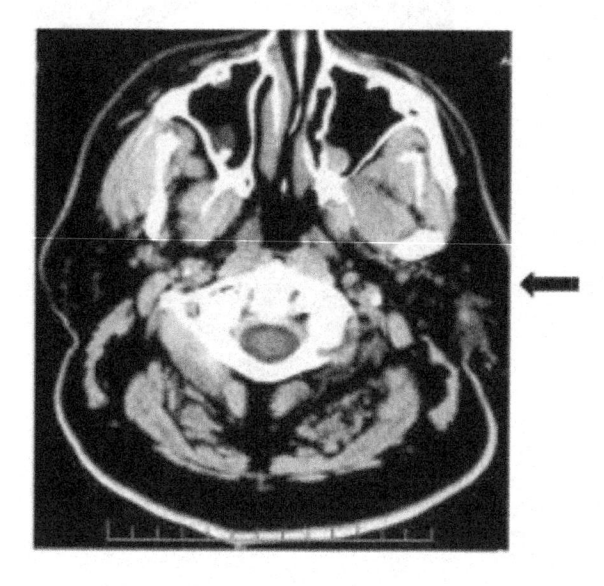

The black arrow show where the bleed happened

Tommy & Karen Drumm

Made in the USA
Columbia, SC
12 April 2019